Drama, Drama, Drama: plays straight outta Oakland

Judy Juanita

Equidistance Press
Oakland

Drama, Drama, Drama: plays straight outta Oakland
ISBN: 978-1-7326098-1-5

Copyright © Judy Juanita 2023

All rights reserved. No part of this publication may be reproduced, distributed, or transmitted in any form or by any means, without the prior written permission of the publisher, except in the case of brief quotations in critical reviews and certain other noncommercial uses permitted by copyright law. All films/ performances before an audience, invited or public, are subject to licensing fees. A performance requiring legal authorization and payment of author royalties (licensing fees) means any performance in front of an audience: whether admission is charged or not, if the performance is public or private; for charity or gain. This excludes classroom use and auditions which the author encourages. For performance of any part of this copyrighted work or the whole – at "readings" as well as "performances" – please seek licensing fee information from:

Equidistance Press
490 Lake Park Ave.
P.O. Box 16053
Oakland, CA 94610
whoknewyouknew@gmail.com

www.judyjuanita.com

Illustration: Rini Templeton Memorial Fund

An introductory note from noted theater professional Erin Merritt

"I am the founder and former Artistic Director of Woman's Will, the San Francisco Bay Area's all-female Shakespeare company, which also produced an annual evening of short plays written and directed by women, the 24-Hour Play Fest. Ms. Juanita first participated in the event in 2005. We were so impressed by Ms. Juanita's writing, and in particular her range and ability to write moving work under extreme time constraints, that we invited her to participate for an unprecedented five consecutive years (2005-2009). She was a wonderful team-player who never failed to produce something witty and amusing yet pertinent, and her plays were consistent audience favorites.

"Even in 2016, women's plays get produced rarely, work by women of color hardly at all, and older women's work almost never. Since 2013, I have served on the Playwrights Foundation's Literary Committee, and in our blind-reading of 500 entries a year for our Bay Area Playwrights Festival, women's writing consistently outperforms the entries written by men. One year five of our six picks were by women, yet less than 20% of the plays produced at regional houses are by women and according to The Guardian, only 12% are by people of color.

"I can also attest to Ms. Juanita's value to the community. Her work ethic and attention to detail as well as her writing skills also led me to hire her for a playwriting residency through Woman's Will. In 2008 and 2009, she taught seventh- and eighth-grade English students at an Oakland middle school how to write and stage plays, one an adaptation of a young adult novel and the other a play on a topic of their choosing—children in war. This residency required her to teach to the VAPA standards for Literature and Language Arts as well as Performing Arts for those grade levels in coordination with the classroom teacher, who was to supplement Ms. Juanita's work on the other class days. This involved tremendous coordination with the school, the teachers and our directors. Ms. Juanita created lesson plans that taught the students basic monologue writing, poetry styles and finally how to adapt, write and edit dramatic literature. We filmed the final productions and PBS interviewed the students and teachers about the second year play for a special on children writing about war. It was an immensely satisfying experience for all of us, but more importantly, Ms. Juanita imparted her love of language and writing to these students, 96% of whom were non-Caucasian, and 30% of whom were English Language Learners. Her creative visualization sessions and her intensive editing with them helped them to become more fluent communicators in oral, expository and creative expression and also helped them learn why and care how we use language in different ways.

"Juanita is a gifted, mature artist whose plays have been featured in venues throughout the country. Her work is relevant and needed." (2016, used with permission of Erin Merritt)

Preface

What is an Oakland sensibility? Since I was born in Berkeley, raised and educated in Oakland from the age of five, I come by an Oakland sensibility honestly. It's an amalgam of sheer grit, streetsmart, sass, earthiness, homespun Southern food and downhome sayings, beautiful parks, concrete playgrounds, and a magnificent lake walked by people from all over the world. It's an outlook that produced the Oakland Raiders, the Black Panther Party, Too Short, the Pointer Sisters, Clint Eastwood, MC Hammer, Morrie Turner, Zendaya, Julia Morgan, Joe Morgan, Curt Flood, Tom Hanks, Debbi Fields, Paul Mooney, Mark Curry, Raphael Saadiq, Ted Lange, Ron Dellums, Goapele, Keyshia Cole, Sheila E., En Vogue, Pete Escovedo, Isadora Duncan, Jack London, Tanya Holland, Daveed Diggs, Ryan Coogler, Digital Underground, and Edwin Hawkins. The common link: they're fighters, they spring from the hills and concrete of this city of 400,000± to fight their way up and, dammit, back down if they have to.

That's what the characters in these plays do, fight, fight, fight, with words or actions. They don't take life as a placid adventure. Whether I've set the stage in London, Oakland, New York City, San Francisco, postslavery, or the afterlife, they keep their gloves handy. Like the true residents of Oakland, they recognize that the black crow of death is always close by.

They speak standard English, Ebonics, slang, curse and codeswitch with the best of them, make metaphors when there's no better way to say it, and make others uncomfortable until they see the light.

In "Counter-Terrorism," the homeless truthteller Ann, for example, uses Black dialect and even slave dialect within her monologues, Ann satirizes her fellow blacks in their rush to adopt names from Anglo-Saxon forebears. Because Ann is ragged and on the streets, she is estranged from other blacks, especially the working and middle-class. But, like many characters in these plays, Ann presents her truth.

I hope the actors and readers of these plays explore these characters and make them work hard in classes, auditions, readings, films, Tiktoks, dramatic presentations, etc. That's why they exist.

Table of contents

The Art of Benevolence 3

> A one-act play using four satirical vignettes that push the limits of kindness
>
> *First vignette, "Samaritan-ism"*: a young woman with a vulgar name, Mercy F**k, finds out about rudeness and the protocols of traveling as she goes through airports from London to NYC.
>
> *Second vignette, "The Art of Benevolence"*: a daughter comes home reluctantly to visit her ailing Irish-American mother and encounters her mother's spirit guide.
>
> *Third vignette, "The History of Sweat"*: a farce about fragrance, funk, advertising, and subways throughout the world.
>
> *Fourth vignette, "New York, New York, It's a Helluva of a Town"*: Students at Columbia University trick a professor into using the N-word.
>
> Running time: 70 minutes

Counter-Terrorism. 47

> A one-act play
> A homeless truthteller invades the mind
> of an educated shopaholic after 9/11
> Running time: 60 minutes

Counter-Terrorism 73
An abridged version of the play

> Running time: 10–12 minutes

"Wait Just A Goddam Minute" 81
A Fat Drama in the Space of a Working Lunch

> A 10-minute play
> Two characters (BBW) talk fat
> Running time: 10 minutes

A Moment of Silence **89**
    A one-act play
    A distraught nurse whose teenage son has overdosed
    falls head over heels in love with a duck
    Running time: 40 minutes

Monologues. 117

The Art of Benevolence

The Art of Benevolence

In a contemporary setting, four satirical vignettes push the limits of kindness in mostly public spaces. They are being put on in a black box uptown NYC theatre with an ego-maniacal bully of a NY director and an impassive stage director.

Vignette #1	***Samaritan-ism*** A woman with an unfortunate name that reeks of vulgarity finds out about charitable intentions while traveling from London to NYC
Vignette #2	***The Art of Benevolence*** A daughter comes home reluctantly to visit an ailing mother and encounters her spirit guide
Vignette #3	***The History of Sweat*** A farce about fragrance and subways the world over
Vignette #4	***New York, New York, It's A Helluva Town*** A play About condescension and the use of the n-word by students at Columbia Univ.

Characters (double-casting of 6 or 7 actors who can play each vignette)

In all vignettes
JB, THE HEAD OF THE COMPANY
THE STAGE DIRECTOR

Samaritan-ism [vignette #1]
MERCY F**K
LIMO DRIVER
AIRPORT SECURITY GUARD
PASSENGER
VOICE OVER LOUDSPEAKER
GHOST OF POLONIUS
SAMANTHA
CHI-CHI/ROSENKRANTZ
LI'L KIM [or any celeb fresh from the plastic surgeon's chair]

Benevolence [vignette #2]
MUM, THE MOTHER
TANYA, THE DAUGHTER
MAGGIE, THE CAREGIVER, WHO SPEAKS WITH AN IRISH LILT
CLAIRE, THE SPIRIT GUIDE
CABBIE

The History of Sweat [vignette #3]
DOROTHY
JILL
RACHEL
THE PASSENGER
THE HERO
THE BROADCAST ANNOUNCER
LONDON BOBBIE

New York, New York, It's A Helluva Town [vignette #4]
REVA
PAULETTA
THE PROFESSOR
RANDY
G-MONEY
THE DEAN

The Art of Benevolence

Samaritan-ism *[vignette #1]*

JB
[Whenever JB comes onstage, he speaks with the air of authority]

This is what I want with Samaritan-ism. Speed. Hit it. Don't take an extra second. Hit the gut first, not the brain.

STAGE DIRECTOR
[reads synopsis]
Samaritan-ism. A woman with an obscene name travels from London to New York to get to a do-gooder convention not getting any respect or help along the way.
[calls off the name of the CHARACTERS. As names are read, actors appear and adjust costumes and hats.]
Mercy F**k/Limo Driver; Airport Security Guard/Passenger on transatlantic flight/Voice over JFK Airport loudspeaker/Ghost of Polonius; Samantha/Passenger in JFK Terminal/Chi-Chi/Rosenkrantz/Li'l Kim/ City Driver/Gildenstern

VOICE FROM AIRPORT TERMINAL LOUDSPEAKER:
Last call for passengers leaving Heathrow on flight
31 bound for New York City/Last call flight 31 New York City/All passengers leaving Heathrow for New York City.
[Mercy goes through airport security carrying a backpack and a heart-shaped red basket. She gets frisked. The security guard pays no attention to others, but can't keep his eyes/hands off Mercy.]

SECURITY GUARD
Your visa says Mercy F**k. That's not a nice name.
[He pulls a vibrator out of her backpack]
And this is big enough to be a missile. Is that what it takes to satisfy a Mercy F**k?

MERCY
Miz F**k to you.

SECURITY GUARD
What's that?
[Tries but can't take her red heart-shaped purse.]

MERCY
This belonged to my mother. Good grief.

SECURITY GUARD
You have a mother, eh? I suppose her name is Mother F**k?

MERCY
Yes, it was as a matter of fact. And I'm on my way to a Good Samaritan convention in Manhattan.

SECURITY GUARD
And I'm just doing my job.
[walks off stage. Boarding the plane, Mercy stuffs her backpack under her seat, then sits, heart in hand]

SAMANTHA
[In the seat next to her, a woman sits down]
Hello, I'm Samantha.

MERCY
I'm Mercy. I'm on my way to a do-gooders convention. I'm Mercy F**k.

SAMANTHA
I'm sorry. I'm sorry. That's the English in me; mum's English. We apologize for everything. I'm afraid I didn't get your name properly.

MERCY
First name: Mercy. Last name: F**k.

SAMANTHA
That's a joke, right?

MERCY
No. They say the longer you do something, the more it becomes a part of you. I'm just an extreme example, like doctors who turn into good Samaritans and chop off whole body parts for you, or lawyers who walk into court in their legal briefs- skid marks and all.

SAMANTHA
[squirms and turns to her book]
I see.
[plane begins to rock with turbulence, heads bob up and down, shouting out]

PASSENGER
Jesus! Mercy!

MERCY
[her head up; Samantha's head is down]
You called me?

PASSENGER
Oh F**k!

MERCY
Yes? I'm over here.

PASSENGER
What are you? Nuts?

MERCY
[talks to Samantha who is scared stiff]
You know, in the United States alone, there are more than 100 million volunteers. That's a lot of do-gooding. Ladling soup for the homeless, helping the elderly, candy striping.

SAMANTHA
And you consider your name alongside those things an act of self-lessness?

MERCY
I started out giving mercy f**ks as an adolescent act of charity. Then it became like a perpetual good deed. Now it's a random act of kindness. I'm listed in the phone directory-Mercy F**k-with asterisks of course.
[Their flight lands and they get up to go]

SAMANTHA
[Starts getting her bags together]
Mercy, I've got to go. Nice meeting you.

MERCY
Me too. Well, I'm off to my do-gooding convention in Manhattan. Strictly biz.
[Both get up to go in opposite directions, and talk in asides]

SAMANTHA
A convention in New York. I can't quite see Mercy F**k on a business card.

MERCY
Why is she mumbling my name? Does it strike her as onomato-poetic?
[They're in the terminal at Kennedy Airport. A mad scene.]

VOICE OVER THE LOUDSPEAKER
Please keep children, bags and et cetera with you at all times. Listen carefully for bomb threat alerts and keep your nostrils alert for noxious toxins. We must check all shoes, so please ignore what drifts up from below. FAA regulations. Thank you, travelers.

LIMO DRIVER
[limo driver with dreadlocks holds up a sign, calls Mercy's name. When he says it with his heavy accent, it doesn't sound obscene.]
Mercy F**k. Mercy F**k. Ya Mercy F**k?
[female passerby recoils]
Ya Mercy F**k?

FEMALE PASSERBY
Please don't insult me. You've probably been in this country all of five minutes.
[runs into Chi-Chi, and Chi-Chi runs into MERCY in a collision of accents]

MERCY
Can you help me, please? I'm trying to get to mid-town.

CHI-CHI
[Ignores her]
I'm half-Nigerian.

MERCY
I'm, uh, Mercy F**k. Would you know where the Samaritanism Convention is?

CHI-CHI
Samaritanism. Sounds like a cult. I'm a good Christian.

MERCY
It's a convening of do-gooders.

CHI-CHI
Jesus freaks?

MERCY
People who help those in need.
I'm Mercy F**k because that's how I started helping.

CHI-CHI
That's obscene and unhygienic. STDs. AIDS. And –

MERCY
And babies…sometimes.

CHI-CHI
Who's going to be at this so-called convention?

MERCY
Won't you be my guest and come see?

CHI-CHI
How much will it cost?

MERCY
A good deed. Please?
[Chi-Chi shrugs. The Limo driver finds them]

LIMO DRIVER
Mercy F**k?

CHI-CHI
She's right here.

LIMO DRIVER
Let's get it on; I haven't all day to ride you, Mercy F**k.
[Motions to her to move it along. Mercy follows him, looks at Chi-Chi]

CHI-CHI
Sounds like a con, not a convention.
[They walk off-stage in two different directions. Driver and Mercy seat themselves in the cab, two chairs, dashing through the city.]

MERCY
You're driving like a bat out of hell.

LIMO DRIVER
I get you there. Don't ya worry. Business is business.
[He broadsides a car. Gets out. Starts shaking his fist and yelling obscenities at the other driver]

MERCY
[Shaken, thrown out of seat, scrambles for her red heart]
For heavens' sake.

CITY DRIVER
Oh F**k! I can't afford an accident. F**k!!!

LIMO DRIVER
Yes, she is, and who are you? Look what you've done to my cab... and to Miss Mercy F**k.

CITY DRIVER
I hope she's not hurt.
[Pulls money out of wallet] Here. No police.

LIMO DRIVER
Is this your idea of a helping hand?

CITY DRIVER
I can do a little soft-shoe, moonwalk, but I can't afford to help her. I dunno, Sammy Davis? Stepin Fetchit? Michael Jackson? Usher, anybody black who can dance? I'm illegal. [Dances off]

LIMO DRIVER
[Gets back in cab chair, pats Mercy].
We're going to get to the destination.
[They keep going. They stop]

LIMO DRIVER
Red Light.
[A ghost in a shroud comes and stands in front of the car, face to the audience]
Step aside, fool.

POLONIUS
My name's Polonius. Don't be in such haste. I know its consequences. I too tried to help and all I got was this sword in my heart.
[Starts singing ballad]

MERCY
[nearly passing out, voice weaker, clutching heart.]
Help! Help!
[Polonius draws his sword and lunges towards Mercy]
Why is this old man trying to kill me?

LIMO DRIVER
It's a ghost. It has no physical power. They stand watch at the bridges for the suicide-y people. Old goat.
[Polonius goes off stage. They keep on in taxi.]

LIMO DRIVER
We're getting there. Don't despair, Miss Mercy.
[A pair of men in tights steps in front of the taxi].
What is this foolishness today? Get out of the street, you. What you think, you're ghosts too?

ROSENKRANTZ
Yes, we are. I'm Rosenkrantz.
And he's Gildenstern.

MERCY
And I'm almost dead. What are characters out of Shakespeare doing here?

ROSENKRANTZ
We're trying to get to awf-awf. Can you help us?
[They bogard their way onto the taxi.]
We were on our way to England, ended up on Broadway in our own play.
Now we're minorities again. But out of fashion.

LIMO DRIVER
Get off my cab. Can't you see I already have a fare, you spooky nothings?
[They hang onto the outside of the taxi, determined]

MERCY
I'm on my way to a Good Samaritan convention. Would you like to come?

ROSENKRANTZ
Is it awf-awf? Supposedly we can get work there in perpetuity.

LIMO DRIVER
Do you mean off-Broadway?

ROSENKRANTZ
Yes. Exactly. Awf-awf.

LIMO DRIVER
We passed it back there. You need to go back.
[They jump off the car and go running and shouting "awf-awf" off stage]
Here is the convention center. Miss Mercy, we've arrived.

MERCY
But am I d.o.a?

LIMO DRIVER
Revive your spirits.
[He parks, gets out to help her out, is accosted by rap star Li'l Kim]

LI'L KIM
Limo, are you my limo?

LIMO DRIVER
Not now, miss. Can you not see someone in need? Miss Mercy, get up, stand up, don't give up the fight!

LI'L KIM
I'm Li'l Kim. I have to get to my photo shoot.

MERCY
[Revives enough to recognize a celebrity]
Li'l Kim! Could you autograph me?

LI'L KIM
Of course. What would you like me to write?

MERCY
I know you refused to snitch on your posse. How 'bout No pain, no gain?

LI'L KIM
And to whom?

MERCY
To Mercy F**k.

LI'L KIM
[Starts laughing]
That's a good one. Mercy f**king. An occupational hazard.
[A swarm of paparazzi knocks Mercy down trying to get to Li'l Kim ho forgets about Mercy, drops the pen and paper to pose for the cameras. They go off the stage, Li'l Kim posing away while the cameras click.]

LIMO DRIVER
[Helps Mercy onto her feet, retrieves her red purse, hands it to her]
Ya made it, no thanks to the blowhards along the way.

MERCY
But all thanks to you, kind one. Thank you so much.

LIMO DRIVER
Welcome to New York.

Benevolence [vignette #2]

JB
[He steps onto the stage with two of the actors. They begin putting on period Irish costumes.]
Play the next one a little slower. Like an offering. It takes time to pull this goddam benevolence out of your wallet.

STAGE DIRECTOR
Okay. The setting is Mum's house. The living room. Characters are Mum the mother, Tanya the daughter, Maggie, the caregiver, who speaks with an Irish lilt, Claire the ghost–

CLAIRE
Excuse me, ghost is a politically incorrect slur against the dead. I'm a spirit guide.

STAGE DIRECTOR
I'm sorry. Spirit guide. How could I have missed that?
Claire the spirit guide, and once again a cabbie.
[turns to JB, speaks with sarcasm]
Don't you have characters who serve the same function throughout?

JB
Stock characters. Vanilla, chocolate, no tutti frutti. In this production, they're all the people who are unintentionally kind or unintentionally mean.

CLAIRE
Mamnoon
[flirtatious].

STAGE DIRECTOR
Merci
[flirts back]

CLAIRE
Gracias.

STAGE DIRECTOR
Merci beaucoup.

JB
Get a room. Jesus! Cut the crap.

TANYA
[Tanya enters the room s.l., bubbly with an air of happy anticipation, carrying her closed umbrella, lightly shaking off the drops of water.]
Mother?
[Looks past the room, as if her mother might be in the back for a moment]
Mother, I'm home. I need a ten to tip the airport cabbie. He's got my bags hostage.
[MAGGIE comes from s. r., a feather duster tucked under her arm, wrapping the cord around an iron, careful not to touch where it's hot]

JB
[visble standing slightly off stage.]
I don't want any of that fake Irish Spring "And I like it too" bullshit.

MAGGIE
Shush. You'll wake her.

TANYA
Who are you, in my mother's house?

MAGGIE
I work for the missus now. And she's just been put to sleep, if you please.

TANYA
What kind of work?

MAGGIE
I'm her caregiver, her home health aide.

TANYA
And what were you doing with her things, about to walk out with them?

MAGGIE
No, not at all. I set to dusting as soon as mam nods away.
[She sets the iron on the table, and begins to dust shelves and ceiling crevices. Mum enters, s.r. She is a bit bent over, still flexible, but it's an obvious strain.]

MUM
Oh my. Tanya, I didn't know who Maggie was talking to. You made it. What an unexpected pleasure.
[A voice is heard from outside, s.l., and two loud knocks]

CABBIE [VOICE OFF-STAGE]
I can't double-park all day.
[Maggie goes off stage right, humming an Irish tune, dusting away.]

TANYA
[Shouts to cabbie]
Just a minute.
[Points in the direction of MAGGIE] Who is she?

MUM
My lifesaver.
[More loud knocks]
Oh, for heaven sakes, who is it?
[Hobbles over and opens the door. A cabbie, with a Giants cap on, steps in.]

TANYA
It's the cabbie. I owe the tip. And why a home health aide?

MUM
Dratted multiple sclerosis. Kicked in again.

TANYA
Mother, why didn't you let me know?

CABBIE
Damn suburban fares, more trouble than they're worth.

TANYA
[Mutters, but she really wants her mother to hear.]
MS, a little flare-up. That makes for a nice homecoming.

MUM
It's not so little.

TANYA
Then why not let me know? In advance of coming home.

MUM
I actually didn't think you were coming. You put off coming twice already.
[Cabbie folds arms, extremely irritated, exhales loudly. Tanya goes to a brown fur coat hanging and goes through the pockets. She comes up with some dollar bills and hands them to the cabbie.]

TANYA
I couldn't get the time off, Mother. [To cabbie.] Please just leave my bags on the porch.

CABBIE
Do you one better; leave em on the sidewalk. [Mutters and walks off stage.] Better yet, the gutter.

MAGGIE
[MAGGIE comes back in, bustling around MUM.]
Now, mam, didn't I tell you I make up your bed whenever you get up from it? My dad argued all my teen years because I said, why make it up when I just have to get back in it at night? But Papa said I needed to make up my bed so no ghosts get in it during the day.

MUM
Oh, I suppose I better listen to you before you drag Claire in here. [Turns to Tanya.] Claire is my spirit guide. We have a whole host of Irish spirits in the house with us. They're good company.
[Tanya shakes her head; she goes to get her bags. Opens the door.]

TANYA
The darned cabbie put them here anyway. Unbelievable! What a grumbler. I'll unpack later.
[MAGGIE begins singing and straightening up a rack of fancy clothes]

MAGGIE
And Mam, speaking of Claire, Miss Claire said to make up your bed tightly as soon as you rise. She said, you're vulnerable, and it's not men she's worried about, it's other spirits. If your hubby comes back to visit, that's all right. It's his bed but men in the great space don't have the power they have here. They get lonely in the great space and meddlesome. Not like here where they just go and conquer.

TANYA
Those are Mother's earliest designs. They shouldn't be handled. They're not clothes. They're history. They're valuable. Do you even know what a textile designer is?

MUM
She knows. She knows. No matter how depressed I am, we make a ritual of making the bed. I always made the bed before but since your dad passed, it's taken on a new meaning. A way to start the day...with some control.

MAGGIE
Mam, good people need to learn how to preserve themselves. When bad people give out, nobody misses them. When good people give out, it's hard on everybody.

MUM
[MUM hobbles over to flowers in a makeshift vase, smells them, then hobbles out of the room.]
I'm down for my nap.

MAGGIE
And I'll take my sit-down along with you, mam.
[Sits down in a chair, a ball of yarn in her lap. Tanya keeps fingering the clothes as if MAGGIE has violated them. Claire enters

the room. She doesn't necessarily look otherworldly but moves very quickly. Neither of the women sees her. She begins fiddling with the clothes, moving them around behind Tanya's back. Tanya goes over to one side of the rack, angered.]

TANYA
As I said, these shouldn't be handled. They're not clothes.

MAGGIE
I haven't touched a thing.

TANYA
Yes, you did. I put this ball gown over here. And now it's in a different spot.

MAGGIE
It's Miss Claire. She's here.

TANYA
And who, pray tell, is Claire? Spirit people. Such nonsense.

MAGGIE
If you still yourself, you can hear her. Did you know that the sense of hearing is the last sense to go? Even after their heart stops beating, a dead person, they can still hear.
[Tanya sits for a minute. She hears a faint singing by Claire, but is unconvinced. The singing grows a bit louder.]

TANYA
I suppose next we'll have a séance.

MAGGIE
Miss Claire said for you to check the records, taxes, and that you have to dig deep, but it's necessary to get dates and figures right. She keeps stressing that this is vital. She also said that this is the way mam and you are going to dig out of the depression– by taking care of records, papers.

TANYA
How would this Claire know I'm depressed?

CLAIRE
I got a visual of her digging near a rose bush or a trellis.
[Tanya can't hear her, but MAGGIE can.]

MAGGIE
She's getting a visual of you digging near a rose bush or a trellis.

TANYA
My terrace has a rose bush and trellises. But that's common. As are dead relatives.

CLAIRE
Things that are written are read by all. Things that are spoken fill the air. And what's in your heart travels faster than anything.
[Claire walks around and they face each other. Tanya reaches out and touches her, has a strong reaction.]
You need to take the phone out of your bedroom.

TANYA
Friends, relatives, even acquaintances call at all hours. To be called after 10 p.m., I …it's always a request that I listen to a problem, get something, do something.

CLAIRE
Look around and see where you can cut over-giving.

TANYA
Overgiving. That's me. Everywhere I go I'm expected to do something, to give of myself. I feel selfish if I don't.

CLAIRE
Cut over-giving. Then you'll feel really good about the ones you choose to be kind to. It's a law. When you violate it, you get fined with rudeness and cruel behavior from others.

TANYA
[Thinks about it] So can you solve my partner problems too? Can you explain why someone leaves after five years with no warning, no regrets?

CLAIRE
He said he was afraid of your wrath.

TANYA
Wrath. I am not an angry person. I am a depressed person.
[Tanya goes from center stage to the left and shouts to Maggie]
Why is this happening?

CLAIRE
We're from the same tribe.

TANYA
I can't believe you. That's odd.
[As if shamed, she bows her head]
I've just been reading about how all the problems in the world started when we went from tribes to nation-states with, in a sense, manufactured animosities, not the more natural fights between the tribes…I am the problem?

CLAIRE
There's more. You have a fear of flying; you want to go to a reunion in LA, but can't because of fear. You can overcome this fear instantly. Have you ever wondered why you have so many problems with airports? The bathrooms don't work, the ones you use. The porters are rude to you. The cabbies, the seatmates who talk nonstop. Your fear is not airplanes but airports. If you can learn the art of kindness, when to practice it, when not, you won't have to tip so much. A simple thank you and less cash splashed around will help you have a smooth journey. Not only at airports.
[Mum comes back in, rested from her nap, followed by Maggie.]

MUM
Dear, did you spend some quality time with the spirits?

TANYA
I guess you'd call it that.

MUM
Most importantly, did you thank them?

TANYA
They're dead!

CLAIRE
Mahalo? Arigato, spasibo, salamot?
[Claire walks off stage, shaking her head at TANYA's ingratitude.]

MUM
Doesn't make a bit of difference. They have feelings too. One day, when I let out a curse word to Claire, she said:

CLAIRE'S VOICE OFFSTAGE
I'm not a god. I'm not a devil. I'm Claire. Merci. Efcharisto. Grazie.

MUM
[Also bows to Claire, to her daughter, to Maggie as she says thank you in a variety of accents.]
Arigato. Danke. Grazie. Merci. Tapadh leat. Bayarlalaa. Mamnoon. Dear, would it hurt to say it? It's not a banknote. It's not a job. It's an expression.

TANYA
Thank you.

MUM
Not to me, to her.

TANYA
Okay, ghost lady, thank you for helping Mum out.

MUM
That sounds like the way people say, I'm sorry if I offended you.

TANYA
Mother, I can only take this so far.

MUM
Thank you is far enough.

TANYA
Okay. Thank you, merci, mahalo, gracias, arigato.

MUM
That's sufficient, dear.
[JB and Stage Director come back on. Actors leave stage left and others come on s.r.]

The History of Sweat [vignette #3]

JB

Nice tempo. I want to show Mercy Fuck getting the short end of things as a backdrop against Benevolence. Can we get the Mercy Fuck actor out here with her little red heart. This benevolence borders on the maudlin. Mercy shows what the absence of kindness looks like.

STAGE DIRECTOR
Get her out here to do what?

JB
Something with that little red heart. Dance, walk across the stage, show her ass, asshole. Can we get this together yesterday?

STAGE DIRECTOR
Not unless she can clone herself. She's already in Benevolence.

JB
Just an idea. Keep it in mind. We gotta move the next one faster. But that was okay.

STAGE DIRECTOR
[reads and, once again, the actors respond when s/he calls the characters names]
The History of Sweat. The characters- Dorothy, Jill, Rachel -are working on a perfume ad campaign for a new fragrance called FiFi.

DOROTHY
[looking through portfolio sketches.]
I say make it as funky as sweat. These are not the Academy Awards.

JILL
Screw FiFi, we're not lobbyists for the fragrance industry. We do underground graffiti.

RACHEL
We are the droplets in the history of sweat. The overpowering eau de fear. The underrepresented fragrances. Not, mind you, those rough facsimiles, scents and oils sold in strip malls and flea markets.

DOROTHY
The scent of butt crack.

RACHEL
Whoa!

JILL
The smell of defeat. The stench of success. The acrid shot up your nose of Rich.

DOROTHY
The rich?

RACHEL
Richmond, California, baby. Totally FiFi.

DOROTHY
[Holds cloth to her nose, coughing as from pollution]
Ugh. Poor people, Not palatable because they're too palpable. You don't want the bottom of the fragrance totem pole.

JILL
Just put it in a montage. Anything looks important if it's in a montage.

RACHEL
Throughout history, aside from regular washing, the only effective deodorant was perfume, until Mum was invented in the 1840s. That's 18 centuries of sweat.

DOROTHY
The Greek physician, Empedocles, made experiments with his clepsydra.

JILL
His what???

DOROTHY
His clepsydra!

JILL
No obscenities in this presentation. It's network.

DOROTHY
His clepsydra. His water clock.

JILL
What the heck?

DOROTHY
[making a power point presentation]
He experimented with his clepsydra and found that when the blood moves up and down the blood vessels, invisible airs and vapors squeeze out or are drawn in. Voila- respiration.

RACHEL
[Rachel takes over and slows down at points to make it clear. Like an airline stewardess, Jill mimes the words babies, all over distinctive scent, armpit, anus and nipples, childhood, puberty and old age.]
Two glands produce human sweat. The first, the apocrine, exists over the entire body at birth, giving babies their all over distinctive scent. Most of these disappear, except for the glands around the armpit, anus and nipples. The glands are usually inactive during childhood, function in puberty, spurred on by hormones. In old age, they wither.

DOROTHY
But sweat is best experienced on subways the world over. Subway stench. The best, absolute best way to know your fellow homo sapiens. Smashed up against them.

J

JILL
And then there's the Dublin subway. And I like it too
[mimics the commercial].
The DART line runs north and south of Dublin along the coast And I like it too.

JB
[Runs onstage.]
No fake Irish. Get it right.
[goes back off, shaking his head.]

RACHEL
And this brings us to the scent of fear. The New York City Subway, 5,000,000 riders. 24/7 muggers, rapists, murderers, thieves, pickpockets, gangbangers, Mafia, thugs.

DOROTHY
And your average Joe, who now has made it par for the course to rescue one's fellow traveler from beneath the wheels of a No. 1 train. Herewith a demonstration of sweat, fear and instantaneous courage.
[Rachel and Jill mimic subway passenger having an asthma attack and falling off the platform whereupon the hero with a cape flourish falls down on her.]

HERO
Don't breathe.

THE PASSENGER
I can't breathe.

HERO
Don't move

THE PASSENGER
I can't move

HERO
This is death.

THE PASSENGER
Is it a die-in?

STAGE DIRECTOR
The train passes over them. They pray loudly. The train goes.

A WOMAN BYSTANDER
Oh my god. You saved your fellow human being. Can I get your autograph? I peed my pants.

STAGE DIRECTOR
They get up. They become famous. One puts on a jester hat. The woman bystander becomes a broadcast journalist. She holds up a cross as a microphone. One of them plays a ukelele badly but the broadcast journalist holds up the cross to it.

BROADCAST JOURNALIST
[sincerely, almost weeping]
I am going to make inane babble about how beautiful it all is.
[a beat]

JILL
Real sweat, take five. The London Underground. Real FiFi.

STAGE DIRECTOR
A British constable in a bobbie's cape, comes through, chasing a would-be terrorist who looks like a nice Indian grandma.

JILL
Sweat personified. FiFi to the nth degree.

LONDON BOBBIE
Stop! In the name of the Commonwealth!

RACHEL
I am a good Indian woman, a grandmother.

LONDON BOBBIE
Open up your coat. Take off your dress.

RACHEL
I beg your pardon.

STAGE DIRECTOR
The bobbie continues to inspect the Indian grandma rudely. She fusses and protests in a heavy Indian accent, snatches her coat back.

RACHEL
This is authentic Persian handmade.

LONDON BOBBIE
You could conceal a bomb in there. If you can't police your own community and control your sons, we will.

STAGE DIRECTOR
The bobbie and the Indian grandma do a strange dance of capture and release, cat and mouse, accusation and shame at being accused, then they go to opposite ends of the stage, i.e. the train station.

JILL
Who's sweating now? The perpetrator or the perp? Same thing, no difference? Hmm.

DOROTHY
FiFi my foot. This is the scent of the sweat of a Slav. I'll show you an Eastern European man.

STAGE DIRECTOR
Demonstrate. Mime. Improv a man of that culture exerting himself strenuously; in other words, work up a sweat.

RACHEL
I can do a perfect Stanley Kowalski. I don't drink anything but Jack Daniels and beer, I get to throw my wife around and jump on her.

STAGE DIRECTOR
Get very physical. Even use Jill as the wife.

RACHEL
Then again, I do Bollywood very well…you know with the spices, things can get very sweaty. And I do gay Bollywood even better.

STAGE DIRECTOR
Here you demonstrate either the sex act or gay behaviorism.

RACHEL
[breaks out of character, looks with irritation at the Stage Director] Either or??

JILL
Crazy. I prefer the familiar to the inane. BART, that's my fear of choice.

DOROTHY
BART's okay. At least we don't have to sweat it out in Baltimore where the subway trains look like mobile homes on tracks.

RACHEL
I've been to Baltimore, Dorothy. Their subway trains don't have seats. They removed them to hold more people.

DOROTHY
Sardine sweat. I say, let's do London. The Underground has just one fatal accident for every 300 million journeys. We should be able to do something in the Bay Area, the most conscious place in the world. Like slow the trains down in populated areas.

JILL
Even in areas where they have separated grades, where there are no crossings, people still find ways to get on the tracks. When people are determined to suicide on the tracks, what can you do?

RACHEL
Accidents have been the driving force for humankind.

JILL
My fear of choice is BART and AMTRAK. A highly specialized fear. Pedestrian euthanasia. It happens weekly. It's the only excuse for being late to work other than an earthquake
[as if talking to her boss]
"Some poor fool walked in front of my train."

STAGE DIRECTOR
Rachel as a drunken sailor stumbles across imaginary tracks and is obliterated.
Improvise here.

RACHEL
[as to her boss]
"Somebody walked into my train. I swear."

STAGE DIRECTOR
Dorothy as a person wearing a Cossack hat, carrying a miner's flashlight, talks in a Slavic accent, about how hard life is here in the United States, and how he longs for the USSR. Improvise here. He walks into the train.

RACHEL
"It was a Cossack, I kid you not. He must have lost his way."

STAGE DIRECTOR
An idiot strumming a ukulele sits on the tracks gets creamed.

RACHEL
"I'm not making this up. It was an idiot today. What can I say? Cal Tran tracks are the new Golden Gate Bridge for suicides. I'm paralyzed with fear every morning. I never know what manner of madness will squat in front of my commute. I need a mental health month."

There. Did I make you sweat? "Underrepresented fragrances." Pfft. It's sweat, goddammit. [to Jill] And you're wearing Calvin Klein Euphoria, you faker.

JILL
Nothing is more FiFi than the scent from burning candles. The scent of candles gone amuck that firefighters from Boston to Baltimore and Ohio to Pennsylvania know. The glorious scent of burning flesh wrought by candles from Wal-Mart, flesh wrought from utility companies, Con Ed, PG & E. Please we must illustrate the smell of burning flesh. Every winter, when the temperature hits freezing, on the East Coast, the next day, the very next day, the papers report: "A body was found frozen stiff in a house." Or "Seven children were left home alone with candles to keep them warm. The mother was out partying and came home to find firemen battling the blaze."

RACHEL
We can't go there. Really poor people aren't marketable. It's not artistic. It's not doable. We have to get back to reality. Sweat.

JILL
Let's use reliable sweat– men. Jocks. Construction workers. UPS brown serge sweat.

RACHEL
Fragrances pour le dude. That's our angle. Whew! How many writers does it take to get one idea??!
[The ladies leave; JB and the Stage Director come back on.]

New York, New York, It's A Helluva Town [vignette #4]

JB
I don't think the men-as-reliable-sweat-dude thing works.

STAGE DIRECTOR
That's how the playwright wrote it.

JB
Don't try indignation on me. I DON'T GIVE A SHIT. A script is a set of directions.

STAGE DIRECTOR
These are vignettes about kindness. [He fondles the red heart-purse] How come nobody gets rescued?

JB
A play is a baby in utero. No one knows what the little devil looks like. We are the alchemists who bring it to life. To make that last one work, cartwheels, lots of running to catch the train and dummy bodies falling onto dummy tracks. Violence, violence, the evil twin of kindness.
[He summons a new set of actors onto the stage. They walk on.]
Now for the tricky one. It's all in the accents. New York it up. Talk New York, walk New York, shit New York. Put some garment workers in pushing garment racks.

STAGE DIRECTOR
This is supposed to be near Columbia University. That's not the garment district. It's Harlem…black people, Ricans, Dominicans, some gentrification.

JB
When I worked Broadway, I had women, stars, at my feet, literally. [makes an obscene gesture]
You couldn't sweep the floor I stood on. This is your Broadway. I'm trying you out.

STAGE DIRECTOR
Spasibo. Arigato. Ngiyabonga. Khawp khun. Mahalo.

JB
I have love letters from femme fatales. I worked the ingénue arena. I mentored them.

STAGE DIRECTOR
Next vignette: New York, New York, it's a helluva town. Characters: Reva pronounced REE-vah, Pauletta, THE Professor, Randy, G-Money, the dean. A professor talks to two provocatively dressed young female students in a classroom at Columbia University who chew gum and blow bubbles obnoxiously. They are chattering in New York accents and high-pitched voices, as

oblivious to him as he to them when he gets going on his lecture. When they burst into laughter, they sound like jackdaws.

REVA
[Blows a big bubble. It pops. The two of them crack up. He grimaces.]
This sucks.

PAULETTA
[Shows Reva a text message.]
Check this out, Reva. This was dope as fuck.

THE PROFESSOR
The archaeology of the Fertile Crescent proved the training ground for agricultural technology. This area of the world begat a host of crucial developments—the city, writing, empires, civilization itself.

REVA
God. Is this boring or what?

PAULETTA
Actually I like our text, but he's so in love with his own voice. Fuck. Enough.

REVA
I told Michael about the Fertile Crescent, and where it was-next to the Mediterranean, and he said, "The only fertile crescent I care about is between them thighs, baby."

THE PROFESSOR
Alphabets, ah, the alphabet. As our text exposes, alphabets only arose once in human history, and that was from Semitic language speakers.

REVA
Oh god, here comes the alphabetologist.
[They giggle.]

THE PROFESSOR
The equivalent of a Semitic intellectual hobo -

REVA
[muttering]
Who he calling a ho? He must be talking to you, Pauletta.

THE PROFESSOR
[coming alive because finally he's got their attention]
This hobo tries to mimic the Egyptian system of heiroglyphics but can't quite. So he focuses on creating sounds which work out better if he just strings together a continuous flow of consonants, exactly like that
[points to their mobile devices].
Like texting-only consonants, no vowels.

PAULETTA
You calling us primitive, Prof. Heidenbog? And getting a little anti-Semitic at the same time?

THE PROFESSOR
By no means. The way you talk, the speed that you convey thoughts, the sequential ordering of important and non-important messages– that's sheer human technology.

REVA
You-mean-talking-like-this-so-fast-you-either-know-me-or-gonna-know-me-in-one-sentence?
[She jumps up and moves toward him, erasing the distance between professor and student. He nods and steps back]

THE PROFESSOR
Before 1492 and the invention of the printing press, punctuation was to writing like a cane is to walking. It was for slower speakers.

PAULETTA
Why do you sound like we are back in history? And you're here condemning us?

THE PROFESSOR
It's ironic you can't see I'm complimenting you. Humans in the Silver Age lived for 100 years as infants…and a demonstrably short time as adults. Kill or be killed. And it was over.

REVA
Oh. Killing us with kindness.
[They burst into laughter, but mock him with their hands.]

THE PROFESSOR
[Now his anger is rising]
You come in here like snails, creeping into the halls of academia, unwillingly at that. And you expect me to creep along with you.

PAULETTA
Are you whimpering like a schoolboy?

REVA
Like a schoolboy who can't find a map of the world on New Guinea?

THE PROFESSOR
You mean "who can't find New Guinea on a map of the world."

PAULETTA
[Dances over to professor in a "bump and grind"]
You're complaining. Like a boy who found out his hole has a pocket.

STAGE DIRECTOR
She turns her back to THE PROFESSOR, but her cell faces him. She's recording him.

THE PROFESSOR
Whose pocket has a hole, darn it.

REVA
[dances away]
Are we confusing you, Prof. Heidenbog? I'll show you whose pocket has a hole in it. A burning hole.

STAGE DIRECTOR
She does a very suggestive dance. He tries to look away but is mesmerized. Slowly, getting in the spirit in a nerdy way, he gets up and dances a bit with Reva. When his pelvic area touches her, he practically throws himself away from her, as if repelled by his own erotic move. They laugh uproariously; he is embarrassed.

PAULETTA
Did you see that in New Guinea? Papua?

THE PROFESSOR
I want you both to understand why the world changed in 1492.

REVA
[continues to dance]
We know why. Columbus discovered America.

THE PROFESSOR
[utterly frustrated.]
No! It was because of Guttenberg. The printing press. Human technology. That's the whole point of the first half of our text.

PAULETTA
And it only took two and a half million years.

THE PROFESSOR
[astonished]
How did you know that?

PAULETTA
I did my homework-like a good little snail.

THE PROFESSOR
And I thought I was going to have to turn flips to get you to this.

PAULETTA
Actually you did. They were perfectly executed.
REVA
Perfect. Tweet, tweet and retweet.
[They leave class very happy. He gathers his composure. Two young white guys come in: one is Randy, short; the taller one is G-Money. They have swagger and are listening to hip-hop, which can be heard faintly. They have on caps/hip-hop garb, pants slung low.]

G-MONEY
Hidey, whazzup? You gon bore us again today?

THE PROFESSOR

[ADDRESSES THEM PROFESSORIALLY ALTHOUGH HE IS
YOUNGER THAN THEY ARE IN A WAY.]
Randy, Gabriel.

G-MONEY
Gabriel. Who dat? Some dude named Gabriel who used to suck
his momma's titties? That who you talking bout? That dude is long
gone. And he ain't comin back.

THE PROFESSOR
Gabriel will be back in full force when he starts job hunting and
has to pay back his student loans.

G-MONEY
Man, I don't need to change up to make my dollas holla.

RANDY
[points to his cell]
I got my money maker right here.

THE PROFESSOR
I love it. You did your homework. You're inferring that because
you know technology, you'll be able to master the art of getting
ahead in a technological society.

RANDY
Nah, man. Inference means it took 400 years to get the airplane
from Van Gogh's vision to the Wright Brothas. And it took 400
years for the white man to get his foot off the brothas' neck. So you
ain't gotta kiss butt to make it. You kick butt.

THE PROFESSOR
But you're not a brother.

RANDY
I damn sure ain't what you are.
[Like the females, he begins slyly focusing his cell on the pro-
fessor, moving close enough to record him.]

THE PROFESSOR
You're talking out of both sides of your mouth. What if, let's just say, what if you ended up on Riker's Island or upstate in Clinton? They shave your head– you're back to being a white boy, pure and simple. That's inference on the inside of prison, not like Columbia or the Village where you can pose.

G-MONEY
Whatever. My niggas out here'll protect me.

THE PROFESSOR
My niggahs! So collegial.

RANDY
What you say?

THE PROFESSOR
I said, "my niggahs." You're being collegial. Do you think you'd get away with that in a prison setting?

G-MONEY
Do you think you can get away with it in a collegial setting?
[His cell rings. He answers.]
Yeah, man, I got it. We getting it. Big time.

STAGE DIRECTOR
G-Money hangs up. Nods at Randy who is getting a microphone and hooking it up to put the professor on broadcast behind his back.

JB
Make sure it's obvious that they're taping the asshole professor saying the word nigger.

G-MONEY
You're not dead until you don't answer your cell.
[turns to Randy]
Dude, member that train crash in LA? The rescuers excavating the bodies while the cell phones kept ringing. They didn't answer.
[They laugh.]
That's how they knew somebody was dead. They inferred it.

THE PROFESSOR
Good example. Give me another one.

RANDY
Oh, you want more?
[Turns to G-Money who focuses his cell on the professor.]
You a glutton for punishment. Hit me one mo time? That's whatchu want?

G-MONEY
[turns to Randy but is speaking to both him and

THE PROFESSOR.]
Do you realize the use of the word nigger is nothing but an addiction?

THE PROFESSOR
I don't know where you're going with this.

RANDY
But it's my addiction.

G-MONEY
Here's the 12-step program for nigger addiction.

RANDY
Oh yeah?

G-MONEY
First [turns to THE PROFESSOR], you have to repeat after me. I am addicted to the word nigger. I can't stop using it.

THE PROFESSOR
[As if to go along with it, says it solemnly]
I am addicted to the word nigger. I can't stop using it.

STAGE DIRECTOR
The refrain echoes faintly from the back of the theater, where the audience can hear it, but THE PROFESSOR cannot. His lines keep echoing faintly as if the mike is broadcasting to all the campus but for his classroom.

G-MONEY
I can't help myself. It feels good to say the word nigger.

THE PROFESSOR
I can't help it. It feels good to say the word.

G-MONEY
No. Repeat after me: I can't help myself. It feels good to say-

THE PROFESSOR
[Getting irritated.] Okay! I can't help myself. It feels good to say the word nigger.

G-MONEY
It is supreme belligerence for me to use the word nigger. And everyone knows that living in New York is like getting a BA in belligerence. So as a New Yorker, I'm entitled. On G.P.

THE PROFESSOR
Where's the inference in this?

G-MONEY
To be belligerent enough to use the word nigger today infers you are already at war with the language police, if not with the cultural heritage of people you neither know nor want to know.

THE PROFESSOR
Ok. Experiment over. You've proven your point.

RANDY
Yeah, we did.
[They turn and leave. Out of the professor's earshot, they keep it up]

G-MONEY
[Their voices sound white, with no exaggerated black/hip hop inflections]
Here's inference for a motherfucker. I heard it on the subway going past Bed Sty yesterday. Some Puerto Rican hoochie said, "I hate

Taco Bell. It tastes like dog food." Ghetto restaurant critics! What the fuck! How does she know how dog food tastes? Do they pack dog food in with government cheese these days?

RANDY
Here's another one. This black guy had the nerve to tell me, "Don't get Kentucky Fried out in the suburbs, man. They don't know how to season that shit." What makes his black ass think I'm going to eat that shit in the first place? I'm not a nigga. I'm a wigga. That shit tastes like it's been fried in white bread.
[They crack up and keep walking.]

G-MONEY
Wait till the dean steps on Heidenbog's ass. School's out, motherfucker.

RANDY
[looks back at THE PROFESSOR]
You got chumped, chump!
[They slap hands and leave. THE PROFESSOR stands there. He starts recording his notes in a tape recorder.]

THE PROFESSOR
"Today was a ride into the thicket, as usual, in the blackboard jungle, circa 2009, with the brats from Long Island and Jersey and Queens trying to act like Bebe's kids. As usual. Like I'm some dumb homeless bum standing on the edge of the street, teetering on the brink of extinction."
[Looks up, looks out the window.]
Hmmm. I like that...standing on the edge, teetering on the brink of extinction.
[The dean enters in a suit and tie, holding the cell phone and microphone the students have used to record THE PROFESSOR]

DEAN
Professor Heidenbog – in my office. NOW.
[Dean exits followed by Professor. Stage Director comes back on trailed by actors.]

STAGE DIRECTOR
[He talks to the red heart, sips coffee, grumbles]
Who would've thought kindness takes so much time and energy?
[JB comes back on, scripts in hand, with the two actresses from the beginning of New York, New York, it's a helluva town.]

STAGE DIRECTOR
Done deal, JB?

JB
No way. I want to see how it works to put the college kids right next to Mercy F**k. You know, New York. And I want my ladies and my gentlemen to enunciate Nigaro Nigaro Nigaro like Figaro Figaro Figaro. Got it.

PAULETTA
That is patently offensive. I don't have any lines with the n-word anyway, so it's not my concern.

JB
Offensive? What do you know about offensive? Theater is offensive. It's meant to offend and stimulate. If it doesn't do that, let them watch network TV. Fuck your delicate sense of propriety.
[Reva starts taping him. He's so on a roll he doesn't see what she's doing.]
And fuck you with your privileged tight-ass MFA from NYU. You think that entitles you. You're entitled to be treated exactly like women have always been treated. With something hard and long right up your lily white ass…Forget it. You're out of here.

PAULETTA
You're firing me.

JB
Kicking you out of the production.

PAULETTA
Because I won't sit and listen to your racial profanities?

JB
Whatever you want to call it.

REVA
[talks to Stage Director]
We're Equity. He can't do this to us. You're a fool for putting up with it.
[shows him the taped evidence on her camera.]

STAGE DIRECTOR
[to JB]
They've got it all on tape.

REVA
You are so busted.

JB
What the fuck.
[throws up his hands in disgust]
Let the inmates run the asylum.
[walks off cursing at Stage Director]
You can have this crap on a silver platter. I'm outta here.

STAGE DIRECTOR
[Sings after him]
New York, New York, it's a helluva town.
[All the actors come back on stage. They start fist bumping, slapping hands, high-fiving, bowing, turning flips and saying thank you in the different languages to each other, offstage to JB, and finally to the audience.]

ARIGATO, HVALA, MAHALO, SPASIBO, GRAZIE, MAMNOON, DANKE, DURDALADAWHY, NGIYABONGA, SALAMOT, GRACIAS, MERCI BEAUCOUP, THANK YOU, THANK YOU, THANK YOU.

END PLAY

Counter-Terrorism

Synopsis

Educated shopaholic Tylea and homeless, pontificating Ann share the stage as Ann invades Tylea's mind in this play about identity, sexuality and acknowledging "the other" in troubled times. Each is middle-aged. Tylea, anxious to be a patriotic American after a past of radicalism, talks about her comfortable life and her uncomfortable, powerful attraction to a severely disabled intellectual. Ann holds forth on life on the street, politics and sexuality. When they speak of 9/11, Tylea glosses over true feeling, preferring to respond to the national directive to "shop, purchase, travel." Ann addresses the event and pushes Tylea not to be a bystander in her own life. Tylea struggles to acknowledge an identity beyond what she buys and her suppressed eroticism. When Ann disappears off the street, Tylea is left to face this new self.

Characters

ANN/TYLEA

The parts of Tylea and Ann can be played by the same person or two actors. Tylea is a college lecturer and a shopaholic, Ann a homeless soothsayer. Ann often refers to herself in the third person as An.

Setting: stage can be bare or Tylea can be engulfed by her chi-chi shopping bags full of luxuries. Ann, with her ragged shopping bags full of personal possessions, perches in front of local upscale shopping stores. Set decoration include chi-chi shops as backdrop and The Gap store/logo between the two parts of the stage that these voices share. Street signs say Dream Street and Broke-Down Street.

Spotlight goes up on Tylea, singing "Someone to watch over me."

TYLEA

I love it when it rains. I can get so much good writing done. In my favorite robe, with the fireplace going. So this is how it happened–

ANN
When it rains on the street, the people stay home and the animals come out. T'other night, I was sitting in my doorway watching the street get all wet and glisteny and I nearly got scared cuz I thought I saw a bear rolling around in the street. And An just froze cuz that what you do on the street when you see somepin funny going down. But I heard when you see a bear, be still. So An still. And the bear kept rolling, and then I could see this bear had two tails. And then I could see it wasn't a bear; it was two raccoons making love, rolling around in the wet just like two people. And they kept at it. And you know what they did when they finished. They nuzzled noses, and rubbed heinies and went on about they business.

TYLEA
So this is how it happened. I was in that twin Doubletree Hotel in Portland; with the cheese and the chocolates and the warm chocolate-chip cookie, a big fat one on the bed. And I had eaten it all. And I was tired of walking back and forth between the seminars and my room. There must have been three conferences that weekend– an Africana studies conference; mine was for writers. Let's not mince words; they gave me a room in Siberia and then I'm expected to trot back and forth. Excuse me, I'm human. So instead of going back for the evening seminar I ordered room service and a bottle of Merlot and kicked back.

ANN
Just cuz I'm out here you think I'm pitiful. I could have a million dollars in a mattress. But An not begging, An talking. All the philosophers not in the ivory tower just like not all Christians in church. Get them helicops back to Oakland. This Berkeley. We don't have helicop crime in Berkeley.

TYLEA
My new antidepressant must be too strong. I keep hallucinating a homeless woman…this beautiful Portland view was of a parking lot full of four-wheel drives so I amused myself. I know guys call it jacking off, right? We women have to come up with a word for it-jilling. Jilling around. Jacking off, jilling around. So there I am, pleasantly high, quietly jilling, noises all around me, people in the next room talking over the sound of the TV, toilets flushing, doors

slamming shut. And I just add the sound effects. And I'm thinking as I peel away my tensions, nobody can hear this. So I let go, let it loose, basically lose it. And I get loud. I'm a reformed screamer. You know, I've been to the 12-step meetings and everything…"Hi, my name is Tylea and I'm a screamer." When I finally stopped my yowling, much to my surprise, there was nothing but dead silence around me. Not even TV noise. I lay there waiting to hear something, anything. Please, toilet in Rm. 207, flush. But it was as if time had stopped for me. Did they all go out to dinner? I lay there for a few. Then I heard them, the people next to me, talking in a hushed tone. So they had been there the whole time? And I had put on a show. I felt embarrassed. I sat up and covered my naked butt with the bedspread. Then I realized they weren't yakking it up, they were making love. I went to the bathroom but I could hear them even with the toilet flushing and the faucet running. And they were getting noisier by the minute. They were loud, and crude: "Come on baby, give it to me" and "Sock it to me, big boy." I was appalled. I put on a pair of denim overalls and a red tee and some moccasins. I mean they just got sickening. Did they not realize how thin hotel walls are. I stepped out in the hall where the strangest thing was taking place. Emanating from the rooms on either side of and across from mine were the sounds of love. Loud love! Intense copulation! Fucking! Waves of it rocking the whole area. At the end of the hall, a man started towards me. "What's all the commotion?" he asked me. I put my hand up as if to stop him. But he kept coming. He had the worst limp I've ever seen. It was as if he had to swing the bottom half of his body around with every step. I wanted to stop him from entering the loud love zone but he just kept lurching down the hallway like a human Tilt-a-Whirl. And the people were just fucking their brains out, like tomorrow was never coming. I didn't know what to do or say. He stopped and I saw he had a cane looped into his belt, dragging alongside him. He said, "Is this disturbing you?" Whaa! The cane, the Tilt-a-Whirl, the people fucking like rabbits on viagra. He was so serious I simply shook my head. "Oh please, let the good times roll, I just want a breath of fresh air." So we went outside and he smoked his cigarettes and I breathed in the fresh Portland air. And that's how I met Max …

ANN
[Truck and traffic sounds throughout her talking. She makes obscene gestures to the passing traffic] Max. That's what I like about white people. They keep the same name generation after generation, Max, Max, Max, Max, Henry the first, Henry the second, Henry the eighth. They names is not confusing. They don't care if the little baby look up at em all funny, like Mabel? Why you giving me this tired name again? We do different. We go whichever way we get enslaved. Wha massa name? John? Das my name. We get with the French and we name ourselves Denise, Charmaine, Elouise. We get with the Irish and it's Siobhan, Mickey. We went Swahili, evbody had Cumbuka, emboli-all them names sound like they got booger or booty up in em. Haki Madhubootie. So now we got all these twenty somethings running around with Ay-rab names. Ahmed, Muhammad, Siddiqi. They just sounded different before Sept. 11: Khalid, Abdul, and Hasan. Now it sounds like your grandson is on the 22 Most Wanted List. And if you go to the Post Office and look at the faces, you don't see Amad al-sheik Abdullah. You see Miz Jones' nephew what been living with her since he got out of prison. Or Tommy Green who six feet eight and cain't play basketball. And white folks still naming babies Thomas and Jefferson and George. And here An test. The Mexicans never enslaved us but show me a black baby name José.

TYLEA
I ask Max, "Which conference are you here with?" "Africana Studies." Africana Studies?! I try to be polite. "How are you involved with African studies?" A professor– And how many blacks did you displace to get that job?– presenting a paper on "black McCarthyism, revealing how black radicals can't advance in jobs, in high levels, especially if they're still activists." My hackles go down. At least he's on the right side of things. "McCarthyism on the black side. Nobody likes to talk about it. It's not a popular cause. There's no Huey Newton posing in a peacock chair, Angela Davis is probably in menopause, Eldridge Cleaver is dead, Bobby Seale is gray-haired and talking computer revolution. Can I get a witness?" Can he get a witness? He talks so fast and every sentence has a topic idea in it. I try to keep up with him but he talks like he walks, like a whirling dervish. "Elaine Brown's in Paris, David

Hilliard sold the papers to Stanford. The top layer's taken care of. It's the bottom that's still on the bottom and the middle is scattered all over the land." He talks like he knows I was in the Panther Party and I haven't said anything to him about that. I'm not wearing a beret and a black leather jacket. In the party when we met a white boy like Max who knew all the names, the lingo, where the bodies were buried, the first thing we'd say: He's an agent.

ANN
He a Marxist, damn. Got all those degrees. She stupid sometime. I meet aging hippie Marxists all the time in Berkeley. They drop big bucks in my bucket. Actually I rather mo white folks walk by me cuz black people is cheap. They give me the look, like 'how come you ain't out working for the man like I have to work for the man?' One of my fellas talks with me alla time. Say he's tenured, a Marxist biologist slash botanist. I say, what is that about-butterflies are free and worms are the wretched of the earth?

TYLEA
Then as if Max heard my thoughts, he says, "Tylea Prist. Where'd you get a name like that?"

ANN
He actually not bad looking. Got them big gray clear marble white people eyes, the kind seem like if you touch em they be ice cold.

TYLEA
I've been bothered by two things lately. In my dreams, I see Max, and that's not altogether unpleasant, and then, of all things, this woman from Berkeley where I shop. She's homeless; her name is Ann. I don't know her last name…do homeless people have last names? The first time I saw her I really tripped. Not only is she my height and size, she has the same coloring but she's so ghetto. It's like seeing my evil twin, my homeless doppelganger. It makes you think…. it makes me think…that could be me. Never…I'm too comfort-corrupt. The really weird thing is the hair: whatever way my hair is, Ann's is too. Braids, balls, twists, wig. Am I losing my mind??!!…I'm dying to know how Max got his injury. He did say it was a boating accident. What kind of boat? Off the coast of Mexico? In a lake? Did the foot he lost get caught in the rudder? It

sounds so CIA-ish, so James Bond-ish.

ANN
You have to excuse our people when we get to talking bout boats and ships. We get crazy bout boats and ships. Jump. Go head. Don't drag me down wichou. Some black people still on the slave ship.

TYLEA
I find her mildly entertaining. Her signs show she has a mind. Why can't she get off the street?
[Holds up a sign "NIGGERS, ACCEPT NO EASY VICTORIES."]
This really bothers me. I hate that word being in vogue. It invalidates the centuries of struggle we've been through.

ANN
I use the word anytime I feel like it, many times I been called.

TYLEA
The worst was the time I realized Ann was going to the bathroom in public. I told her, Ann, this is shameless. You can use the bathroom in the store…they'll give me a key and I'll let you in. This is beneath human dignity. This is appalling.

ANN
This is life. Where my handiwipes, Miss SnootyPoot? Get that hoopty off the street. There oughta be a law.

TYLEA
How do you ever expect to change your situation? One of these shopkeepers could be the very one to give you a job.

ANN
The last job I had they wanted little black Sambo. So I was little black Sambo for four days. That's all I could take. Four days… Can't use the word nigguh! In the shelter where I go sometime so my feet won't swell so much I call the ants my nigguhs. Turn on the light, it be so many ants swarming around the sink, I say, 'hello, my nigguhs is here wit me tonight'…sometime they the only company I get.

TYLEA
[Changes to short brown wig.] I was waking up, getting my coffee, organizing my day when my girlfriend called me and said, "Turn on the TV." And it…it was just unbelievable, like a movie. When they kept playing it over and over, the planes crashing into the towers, I was stuck to the sofa like a plastic slipcover. And you know, that was 7:30 in the morning. By 1 pm I had to get out of there. I had to do something. I had to prove to myself that the world wasn't going to blow up in my face. I got on that freeway and drove and drove. I was really afraid. I started going east I guess because how much further west can we get? I kept going and going and somehow and I ended up in front of Saks Fifth Avenue in Walnut Creek.

ANN
Cross Palm Springs with the Stepford Wives and throw in Hong Kong and you got Walnut Creek.

TYLEA
And I shopped. I didn't have a smile on my face. I didn't feel good but I wasn't sitting in my condo going out of my head with anxiety.

ANN
[Looking up at the sky] Where that President? How long you gonna stay up in that plane? Do we still has a government? What we paying you for, Georgie Porgie pudding pie? Get down up them skies and run this show.

TYLEA
Yes, I shopped. I'm a shopper. We do what we do. And, lo and behold, what does the president of the United States eventually tell everyone to do?

ANN
What was the moral advice of duh president of the duh United States? Uh huh.

TYLEA
He said, "Shop, buy, use your credit cards, get on those airplanes, travel." I wasn't that far off the mark. I'm in sync.

ANN
An and An bags got off the Walnut Creek BART and the po-lice escorted me back onto the Walnut Creek BART. But the way they did it made me love they little selves.

TYLEA
I found this new jeweler out in Walnut Springs. Did I say Walnut Springs, I meant Walnut Creek. Just the most gorgeous selection of silver and amber I've ever seen. And I bought this necklace. Isn't it beautiful? The workmanship. And as I bought it, all the events were going on. I thought, these are my worry beads; so every time that I wear it, it's a calming thing-I bought it on 9/11. The detail. Can you imagine the hours, the crafting that went into this?

ANN
She repeating what the saleslady told her. The buy this, buy that Mumbo Jumbo.

TYLEA
And the boxes, I keep all the boxes. They remind me of the joy of the purchase. [fondles the necklace] I had them scale it down just a bit to fit me. It wasn't quite right. So I went back in and we worked with it. I haven't even worn it anywhere. I guess that's when you know you've made it on some level. You have it and you don't flaunt it.

ANN
Those police in Walnut Creek pulled out their wallets and gave An three $20 bills. Sixty dollars to get outta Dodge, oh, they never gave those Southern black boys a dime to catch the next train running. Oh no, it was get out before the sun rises or …you know what. I don't mind going back to Oakland, but I love me some Berkeley. Berkeley is the only place in the universe where white people on the street smile at you and nod, like the way colored greet each other down South. Of course, they most likely high or butt naked or deadheads. Old hippies. I don't mind.

Counter-Terrorism

TYLEA
I have different hair. She has different hair. Possibly she's genuinely psychic, related to Miss Cleo. Maybe she intuits what I'm wearing and just does this to drive me nuts…maybe I'm someone she admires, a role model.

ANN
Some people stuck on stupid, some people stuck on theyself.
An like to think about world events. If the World Trade had happened in Harlem, this would be a different world: "A plane driven by brown men landed in the middle of the Harlem State Office Building, killing hundreds of Harlemites. And, oh my god, missing Bill Clinton by a matter of yards. What were they thinking? Does he have the luck of the Irish or what? The fire engines were late as usual. Who gets to ghetto fires on time?"

TYLEA
So did you hear all the cursing on network TV? The fireman who saw the first plane hit said, HOLY SHIT. And the TV stations played that over and over. HOLY SHIT HOLY SHIT. So that's it? We can curse on network TV now? What happened to the FCC's seven forbidden words that made George Carlin's career? Who cares? Holy shit? The first night David Letterman was back and talking about the attack, he said, the GODDAMN terrorists…

ANN
An trying to figure out why this didn't happen before. Like when Kennedy was killed. OH SHIT. SOMEBODY KILLED THE FUCKING PRESIDENT. DAMN. WHAT HAPPENED? WHO FUCKED UP? Or like "Marilyn Monroe was discovered dead in her fucking bed, can you imagine the look on the damn coroner's face!" Or like down South on the news when Martin Luther King was killed, can you hear it in real life? "Martin Luther Coon was killed. Good. Who took that nigger out?" Break one rule, break all the rules.

TYLEA
How are we going to drive humvies up mountain slopes in Afghanistan and across deserts in Iran when we can't even steer our SUVs on route 80?

ANN
Nigguz I know said they were watching the world trade to see if-

TYLEA
There she goes with the n word again. I never use it.

ANN
Nigguz I know said they were watching the world trade to see if nigguz was jumping out the windows. And you really couldn't tell. And that made folks nervous cuz how you know what to feel if you don't know they color?

TYLEA
One good thing that's happened: those reality programs lost some viewers. And I'm glad. I watched THE FEAR FACTOR this summer, thinking: this is a whole generation that grew up in a peacetime economy. Do they know these things happened in the south, hello, being thrown from bridges, hanging from trees? I'm curious as to the backgrounds of the producers and creators of these shows because these shows are very close to what oppressed and ravaged populations face: Eating worms; Being dragged by ropes on the back of trucks –

ANN
Yello black contestants, have you heard of Jasper, Texas? A black man was dragged to his death there. What? You just want that $50,000. Whatchou say? "You an affirmative action dummy." uh huh.

TYLEA
At least on one show there was a brother and while they dropped contestants into a pit 400 rats ran all over them. But the brother said: I can't go through with this. I'm from New York. I can get rats at home." He retained his dignity.

ANN
An heard bro thinking: "Damn, if only it had been squirrels or turtles, anything but rats. I gotta represent."

TYLEA
Anybody know Eric Benet, the singer? Does he have a resemblance to Osama or what? I'm scared for Eric.

ANN
So here's an open letter to Eric Everybrother.
Dear brother: Do not grow a beard. Do not wear a towel on your head. Do not grow an extra ten inches…FIRST WE TRAIN HIM TO BE A HUMAN ATTACK DOG …AND THEN HE TURNS ON US. Bro, watch out…

TYLEA
So now we're just bomb-crazy. Bomb the terrorists. Get the bombs ready. Crank up the munitions factories. Don't forget they're here. How you gonna bomb Jersey City?

ANN
You might hit the Sopranos.

TYLEA
How you gonna bomb Oakland, an island of eighty dialects?

ANN
How you gonna bomb Florida, a foreign country inside a foreign country?

TYLEA
We are a foreign country Africans Asians Europeans squatting on Cherokee Seminole Creek soil.

ANN & TYLEA
You gonna bomb Trenton? Passaic? Newark? Camden? Just take out New Jersey, right.

TYLEA
Can you smart-bomb Boston and bypass Cambridge? Dearborn and not hit the Grosse Pointes? Fremont, California?

ANN
Oops, we nuked Silicon Valley.

TYLEA
Are you making a smart-bomb with a racial profiling chip?

ANN
Technology's a bitch, ain't he? And An gotta talk about these flags.

TYLEA
And I love flags. I treasure my father's flag. He was a Tuskegee airman, signed up for World War 2 the day after Pearl Harbor. I loved the pictures of Betsy Ross sewing that flag. Even after I learned slaves were in the background sweating and bowing and scraping and weaving in the middle of the night while miss Betsy slept in her bed that they had made, I still loved the flag.

ANN
An still scared of white people collectively. They invented Godzilla.

TYLEA & ANN
Blacks invented the ironing board, the stoplight, blood transfusion, the refrigerator, the roller coaster, the hydraulic shock absorber, the curtain rod, folding chairs, the fountain pen, the fire extinguisher, the wrench, bottle caps, the pressure cooker, the pencil sharpener, and the elevator, all stuff to make life easier. Who invented tear gas and bomber jets? It's the difference between CAN I HELP YOU & CAN I KILL YOU. I have a friend who won't buy a flag. She says, "All these flags are frightening. These people are exhibiting crowd behavior."

ANN
I get scared when white folks go along with the crowd. That's KKK time. They might end up dragging An behind a pick up truck cuz An didn't buy a flag. Here An taste test for patriotism. You an American if you squirm at eating #1. Lassie. 2. Secretariat. 3. meow, and #4. Chittlins. Yep, chitlins, UNAMERICAN.

TYLEA
I had a headache after seeing the planes crash for the fiftieth time.

ANN
I grew up on Emmett Till and JET magazine. Since when did folks get so fucking innocent that they can't see blood and suffering? JET was the only place that would publish the burnt up corpses of the lynched Negroes, the only place where you could see Emmett Till body all laid up in the funeral home, where his mama said, "Let the whole world see what they done to my boy." As I recall, some folk used to hold lynch parties and make picture postcards out of the poor burnt up bodies.

TYLEA [SINGS "I FEEL SO SMOOCHIE"]
I was married once. For a year. This friend approached me when I lived in Gainesville.

ANN
She tripping. Let's get this straight, We have a war on terrorism sponsored by some old hands at terrorism. We had a war on drugs sponsored by the drug companies who flooded us with designer drugs. We had a war on poverty in the 60s and 70s that made rich people even richer in the 80s and 90s. We had Star Wars and the evil empire collapsed and now we have Russian gangsters worse than the MAFIA right up our butts… maybe war is obsolete.

TYLEA
$7500. Somebody wanted to pay $7500 to marry me so he'd be legal. I didn't have to live with him that long. He wasn't even there most of the time.

ANN
Don't cry for me, Argentina. Argentina where they have ten-day presidencies, three days if it hits the fan. We should consider that: Hey, Georgie, you got five days. Stand up to daddy on this Enron shit. Ten-day presidencies make a blowjob look awfully efficient. A three-day presidency makes it mandatory. Is it time for women to take over? No the Margaret Hatcher-Thatcher women. Women.

TYLEA
Is she invading my mind? How could that be? She's poor, black, ornery and homeless.

ANN
Excuse me, miss smarty, black and homeless is redundant. We been homeless for 400.

TYLEA
I'm not taking mind-altering drugs. When I was married, he tried stuff at first. You know, he'd go out to the movies –

ANN
He lik-ed porno movies.

TYLEA
—and he'd come back and wake me up with these truly outrageous suggestions. And I just looked at him, like, "you want me to do what?" I mean he wasn't even a real husband. And he wanted me to do things a real wife wouldn't do! But out of curiosity, years later, when I felt comfortable enough with myself, I ventured into the porno section of the video store –how come it's always sectioned off with these smudgy-dirty curtains -and I rented a porno movie. And then I realized where he, he– had been getting all of those outrageous ideas.

ANN
He, he…Yo hubbin. That what the slaves called they husbands, mah hubbin.

TYLEA
It prevented me from having to file for bankruptcy in 199– - well, the second time.

ANN
And she thinks she all that.

TYLEA
This is unnerving. She can't even get a shopping cart. Why would someone like this be a part of my life, part of my psyche? It doesn't make any sense… Like other women my age, I meet a lot of married men. But I hate dealing with married men.

ANN
Yello. I don't mess with em myself. They nasty. Take yo fishing pole back to the pond where it belong.

TYLEA
And then I meet the Ramen Noodle men. Men who want an Instant Woman, you know, just pour hot water on her and there she is, a woman for you. They're usually settled, even retired, they have all these material goods – house, car, the pension fund, and they just need a woman to fill that slot. They end up calling me in a matter of weeks saying, "I met this wonderful woman. She's my everything. We spend every weekend together since we met."

ANN
Don't leave much time for shopping.

TYLEA
And then I get their Xmas card, Mr. And Mrs…But Max came to town to take a course at The Center for Independent Living. He could conceivably be in a wheelchair so he has to learn how to navigate one.

ANN
An don't see nothing wrong with a man with one foot. I had a girlfriend in a wheelchair. I lifted her little butt onto the bed and we did what we came there to do and I lifted her little butt back off that bed and into her wheelchair and we left that little hotel. She just picky.

TYLEA
I spoke to Max politely but I had to bring it up, "I've shared so much with you. Wouldn't it be strange if you were an agent?" He got mad: "Wouldn't it be smarter if the FBI sent a black agent?" And I said, what would they want with me anyway? I'm not a radical anymore. I work, have perfect credit, don't make U-turns in the middle of the street, pay my parking tickets. On time. It was our first argument.

ANN
Their first argument. You can be picky when you got it good. I had it good. An didn't always be out here like a wild dog. I had a house and a family. My luck got bad and then it disappeared. Nobody wants ya when ya down and out. She just picky. She need to meet the Namibis…I saw these Namibi refugees on TV. Black as midnight. So black they were blue. Beautiful. Stunning Black. And a white lady from Paly Alto was showing them around a park, a nice, big walking and jogging park down there near Stanford. And she was just a showing them how to go walking in this trail that was all winding and getting into darkness. And one of them Namibis said, "Will I get eaten if I go in there?" Ain't that nice? Afraid of lions and tigers. We not afraida lions and tigers. We got bigger problems. Wait till he gets pestered to death by telemarketers. Or has to walk past the homeless. Funk. Dirt. We more scared of dirt than lions and tigers. We got guns and zoos. We tame wild animals. I got things worse than funk but if you never get to know me, you'll never find em.

TYLEA
Max thinks that most of the homeless just need jobs, full employment. I agree.

ANN
Please tell Peg leg Pete Negroes don't wont jobs, they don't wont full employment. Unemployment is self-medication for Negroes. We get fired, "Fuck it. I didn't want this job no way." We would go stark raving mad if all us had to work every day. That demands yo attention. And Negroes don't wanna pay attention cuz when they do they damn near trampled into extinction. We better off unemployed. And An a prime example. An not drowning in credit-card debt. An don't have no phone to get turned off. An mortgage not worrying her to death. And An not getting high blood from trying to keep up with the Joneses. And An ain't had a job since Hector was a pup.

TYLEA
Max calmed down after his rather nasty reaction and said I wasn't paranoid. He suggested I had made a God out of my radical past, something I turn to whenever I need it but something I feared deep down. I decided to investigate, to see if there was some truth to it. And I went to Slim's in San Francisco to see The Last Poets. New York, New York, the big apple, boom boom boom bompboomp. These guys were the super foxes back in the day.

ANN
And onstage they look like fat albert himself. New York, New York, the big apple, boom boom boom bompboomp.

TYLEA
They told the crowd the Hansons' success paid for their tour. The audience was young and white, baby boomers buying the drinks and the younger crowd rushing the stage.

ANN
Everybody gets old.

TYLEA
And I walked Lake Merritt and ran into Ishmael Reed and he nods, and he's so gray I can't believe it. Trying to get in his walk before dark. Just like I was.

ANN
Everybody needs exercise. Even An.

TYLEA
And then I got invited to this luncheon at Angela Davis' house. And I help out with the dishes. And I'm talking to Angela Davis about pottery ware and how to use the dishwasher. Angela Davis!!

ANN
Everybody got dishes to wash, cept An. TYLEA
And I went to this soiree with some black arts people and it was for Kwanzaa. And after dinner, they broke out the cocaine, right in front of their teenager. I was shocked. And the host said, "You were in the Panthers. I know you did this." Yes, 30 years ago, and not in front of kids.

ANN
How real is Kwanzaa when Negroes buy the cards from Hallmark at the Walgreen's?

TYLEA
Maybe the past is my rosary. [Puts on new wig.] She can't possibly have the scarf selection I have. Why is peace so inconceivable? If peace is inconceivable, so are we.

ANN
While you working so hard to stay afloat, I got time to read the New York Times. It say we killed 8,000 to 12,000 Taliban fighters and maybe 1,000 afghani people. But yo prez say military intervention is justified because if all go well, uh huh, the child and infant mortality rates will drop. There will be 112,000 fewer children dying and 7,500 fewer pregnant women dying. In other words, you didn't die; we stopped you from dying before you were even born. They call it preventable deaths. So war is justified. O bootiful for spacious skies.

TYLEA
There's an old saying: even if you have a reason to go to war, you shouldn't. She has acrylics. How can homeless get $40 nail jobs?

ANN
Cuz the Korean take my money which ain't marked homeless. Still stuck on herself instead of the bigger problem. The man got in the Presidency ass backwards in the first place. Stole it fair and square...did lap dancing for those corporate peoples who gave him so much money. You notice they lined up for they corporate welfare checks the minute the smoke from the towers cleared. Where my 15 billion? Pay me, Uncle Sam. And again one little black woman, first Miss Barbara Lee stood up and said, No you can't have a blank check, and then that congressher from Texas stood up to em, too, when the airlines wanted they welfare check and said, wait a minute, wait a minute, how we knows you ain't gonna take this money and pay your people and then the taxpayers have to foot the bill?

TYLEA
Sex, sex, sex brings out all our idiosyncrasies, the little quirks. One of mine is doors. I must have doors shut, drawers shut, closet doors shut. I just can't do it if the door is open. I've been known to stop everything and get up and shut the door. Why? I'm not Freud. I don't know. Then I met this brother who could not function without a clear glass of water next to the bed. Period. Sex. Water. Clear glass. No ifs, ands or buts. And there I am with the doors. And I got it. All this jumping up and down. Insertion, removal, insertion, removal. Put it in, put it in, take it out, take it out, ooh baby, ooh baby. It increases the friction…it's exciting. Coitus interruptus. It's been a month of Sundays since I met an intelligent literate man with no quirks.

ANN
When was the last time she had some?

TYLEA
[Begins to wash her feet ritualistically] I always take care with my feet when I'm about to have sex. I mean it's so elemental. There you are with your feet up in the air-you do not want them to smell [looks at her feet as if for the first time] Oh my god, I forgot, I have flat feet. What is he going to think?

ANN
He got one foot. A foot. Do you think he give a damn?

TYLEA
[sings more of the song, "although he may not be the man some girls think of as handsome, to my heart he carries the key. Won't you tell him please to put on some speed, follow my lead, oh how I need someone to watch over me" and wraps herself in a blanket shawl, jumping around, happy] That was the friendliest sex I ever had in my life.

ANN
Friendly?? You know she crossed the color line cuz bro get ferocious when they fuck … bro gotta represent. They represent they family, other brothers, your former lovers, black history. Hollywood show you how white men fuck ON TABLES & STAIRS

& HARD SURFACES, ON DESKS & MARBLE STAIRCASES. Please!! Do not attempt to fuck a bro on a futon. Bro gotta be active, bro gotta move. To fuck bro, you need air bag, mattresses, foam, waterbed, Sealy Posturepedic. And you best have a chiropractor in the next room. Brothers work at fucking. They may say fuck work but they work at fucking.

TYLEA
[still ecstatic, picks up a scarf] I love this. A hint of Africana. Not too much. Being African-American is like a spice. Don't overwhelm the whole dish…

ANN
Where do a billion dollar come from? The same place a dollar come from. Somebody's blood, sweat and tears. And what America gon look like after ten years of these billion dollar wars: See An just a precursor. A precursor. That don't mean I'm a little bitty cursing woman. It'll be homeless all over. Sleeping in yo front yard. Pissing and pooping in the hedges and the streets. Rich people off in gated communities. The rest of y'all together. You think it's such a big distinction between me and you. No middle-class. No poor. Just the rest of y'all. An not communist. An a realist. Somebody have to pay for war. And it ain't gon be the rich. They make money from war. YELLO. Tell Georgie to send his darling drunken daughters into those helicopters with they butts dropping out of the helicopts onto the dessert. Ain't gon happen. No, you send yo children to fight. And the rich man see a gold bullion in each body bag that come back. And you think yo schools a mess now.

TYLEA
I don't believe in doomsday predictions.

ANN
"We can fight two wars at the same time." Yeah and you know who baby boys gon be on point. They last name won't be Rumfeld. Why do they hate us? How come I never hear any black people saying that? Why do they hate us? How bout Eagle-Pilcher what made them stupid batteries for the smart bombs? Why do they hate us? Ask the farmers in Putumayo about Plan Colombia. Why do they

hate us? Try HUNGER! BOGARD!! SELFISH!!! Why do they hate us? Because you're oblibious!!!!

TYLEA
She's inhabiting me. [puts on a green wig] This should stop the craziness. She can't possibly have a day glow wig. Even if she had the money, how would she select a green one? If she does, it means she is, in fact, a figment of my imagination. All I have to do is not imagine…After sex, I'm wide awake. Max is snoring but lightly, not foghorn snoring. I'm about to drift off. As I close my eyes he wakes up. I feel him look over at me. He thinks I'm sleep. I try to keep my breathing soft and regular. He slides out of the covers and the bed. I want to say, Wait, I'll help you. But he's on the floor so fast. I can't believe it. He's crawling on his hands and knees. Without moving anything but my eyelids I watch him. I can make out his naked white butt bobbing along.

ANN
He looks like a baboon.

TYLEA
He goes to the bathroom and he grunts and he must be grabbing hold of the tub, pulling himself up. I hear his one foot hit the tile floor.

ANN
He peeing. And who you trying to fool with a green wig? You look like you shot yourself.

TYLEA
I was always torn about having been in the Party. Max and I talked about it. On the one hand, geez, it was so exciting. I was there. I did it. I carried a gun in my purse. I mean, it was just a little .22 and I worked in the post office by night and lived in a safe house by day. On the other hand, people died. I was so silly. People were killed, murdered, set up, maimed, imprisoned, and ruined for life. It wasn't a tea party. In 1975, the murder rate in Detroit was the highest. I felt responsible. Like I had taught the masses to pick up the gun and then they turned it inward. …I was 21. What did I know? Well, I knew something. I knew there was injustice. And we

did something valuable about it. We spotlighted it. Now I'd rather laugh cry write my stories.

ANN
She ain't gonna mention all the fucking that was going on. She got selective amnesia 'bout that.

TYLEA
Max said the real value of revolutionary organizations is their residual effect. So the Panthers were active for 10 or so years, But 15 years later, the whole county, the world, sees Rodney King getting beaten by the LAPD –

ANN
OH WHAT AN ASS-WHOPPING

TYLEA
Is she in my body now? [tried to exorcise Ann]But because of the party, they have the framework to understand police brutality. My own mother who grew up in the South cried her heart out to see the video on the news. And I said to Mom, "Mom, this is why we did what we did in the Black Panthers," and she said, "Yes, but to see it in front of my very eyes is another thing." Max said revolutionaries exist in their moment. They change the social order and they're extinct. [epiphany]. Wow.

ANN
Intellectual mumbo-jumbo. What she mean is every dog have his day.

TYLEA
He said I have a museum in my mind.

ANN
She in love.

TYLEA
I am not.

ANN
She ain't. Do credit cards fall in love? Do American Express hoochie-coochie with the Discover card?

TYLEA
Oh my gosh, I'm channeling Ann.

ANN
She gotta love herself fore she loves somebody else. Max. Hmmph. Max remind me of a white woman I know, one a' my buddies... she big, got dishwater hair. On Sunday, she go up and down where the black churches are. First she go inside the open front door and estimate where in the service the pastor is. She know bout call and response. She know where the climax. Then she walks out wif her cane and her waddle. She bold. She go round the back door and check to see if it's a feast waiting for the Sunday go-to-meeting folk. Cuz she know bout black churches. [starts singing "Amazing Grace"] A-maz, white folk church over, Zing, White folk be out the door, Grace, white folk be at the Sizzler eating dinner, How Sweet, it Monday morn, white folk at work, The sound, white folk be done got they paycheck and black folk still in church. And she help herself and keep on down street, as resolute as a street dog. She been doing this for years, say her only good meal is on Sunday morning in the black community.

TYLEA
You know sometimes I'm leery of the homeless until I go on a diet. Then I realize somebody who hasn't eaten three squares, hasn't slept on comfy pillows, has more to fear from me than I have from her. Even after 9/11, I don't know if it's being in California. But being American still means being invincible. My girlfriend from back East e-mailed me about some threat to the nuke plants in the Bay Area…she wrote, "Tylea, I'm so alarmed. This tip comes from a former CIA director in conjunction with a very well-established Los Angeles psychic." So that makes me feel just as secure as before.

ANN
People think men are from Mars and women are from Venus and the homeless from Pluto. People don't like us cuz we down on our luck. You wanna do urban renewal on An. Whatchou gon do when half the population is homeless? When you finish paying for this war and that war, that's what gon happen. [starts fending off blows] Do it make you feel good to beat An? You can wipe up the street with An. Kick me till I'm down. An not going nowhere. An goin be here for a while. Why you kids wanna mess with An? [screams and stumbles from the blows] How you kids get so mean? Y'all ain't Berkeley kids. They high. They mellow. Police! Police! I want to report people brutality. People brutality!
[Ann stumbles off]

TYLEA
Oh my god, Bermuda is lovely. I didn't feel what they say about some distinction between the black people who live in Bermuda and the black tourists. I'm feeling great. I got a tan. [rings a shopkeeper's bell] Have you seen Ann? I got a promotion-wanted to give Ann $20. Haven't been down here in a month. On vacation in Bermuda. I missed her. She's so down to earth and gutsy. Ann keeps it real, compared to what. Ann? Gone? Where? What do you mean, they put her away? You talk like that about dogs. Ann is a survivor. Maybe I should check the shelters… Patrolman Dan identified her? She was beaten to a bloody pulp. Ann? Who would beat Ann? Why? For the heck of it. What good did that do, beating Ann senseless? I don't understand. [Walks over to Ann's signs] Don't take her stuff out, I like her stuff. I don't like it. But I want this sign. [Picks up "Niggers. Accept no easy victories."] I used to hate this.[she covers up the word "Niggers" with her hand] African-Americans, accept no easy victories. Oh, Ann.

ANN
[puts on a pair of droopy wings] It's that hard to imagine An with wings. I thought all God's chillums had wings. May I remind you the KKK were evil as hell. And heaven's not all it's cracked up to be. It's crowded like Disney World… And Abraham Lincoln hit on me. You did the Emancipation Proclamation. I know, I'm black. And he say, how can I tell? And oh my god, Martin Luther King Jr. I never thought I would be…excuse me, what about your dream? It came true. In color. On TV. All the children, all different races, all levels of ignorance and stupidity telling all their business to the entire world. Ricki, Jerry, Oprah, Sally, white, black, stupid, smart, young, old, Midwest, south, breaking bread together the night before in their hotel rooms, busting heads the next day. Your torchbearers. …Let's catch up? Jesse Jackson had a baby out of wedlock…all in a day's work? The Republicans are in the White House…you love a good fight? Your children want to turn your center into Graceland…everything is instructive? Some people think your legacy is tarnished… great ideas have periods of praise and decline? OK. Al Sharpton is running for President…Whoa, Martin Luther King Jr. slipped off the pinhead. He's falling in space. I've lost contact.[Ann runs off-stage to find him, her voice dying out] He's in the stratosphere. He says he being reincarnated …as a crack baby who will be adopted by aging progressives who will raise…HER!!!?? to make a difference again. Again. And again. That's all, folks.

THE END

Counter-Terrorism

An abridged version of the play

Counter-Terrorism: An abridged version

TYLEA
On 9/11, I was waking up, getting my coffee, organizing my day when my girlfriend called me, "Turn on the TV." And it…it was like a movie. They kept playing it over and over, the planes crashing into the towers, I was stuck to the sofa like a plastic slip-cover. And you know, that was 7:30 in the morning. By 1 pm I had to get out of there. I had to do something. I had to prove to myself that the world wasn't going to blow up in my face. I got on that freeway and drove and drove. I was really afraid. I started going east I guess because how much further west can we get? I kept going and going and somehow I ended up in front of the Saks Fifth Avenue in Walnut Creek.

ANN
Cross Palm Springs with the Stepford Wives and throw in Hong Kong and you got Walnut Creek.

TYLEA
And I shopped. I didn't have a smile on my face. I didn't feel good but I wasn't sitting in my condo going out of my head with anxiety.

ANN
Where that President? You in that plane for 9/11, back in it for Katrina. What were we paying you for, Georgie Porgie? Pudding pie?

TYLEA
Yes, I shopped. I'm a shopper. We do what we do. And, lo and behold, what did the president of the United States eventually tell everyone to do?

ANN
What was the moral advice of that long-gone president? Uh huh.

TYLEA
He said, "Shop, buy, use your credit cards, get on those airplanes." I was in sync.

ANN
An and An bags got off the Walnut Creek BART and the po-lice escorted me back onto the Walnut Creek BART. But the way they did it made me love they little selves.

TYLEA
Just the most gorgeous selection of silver and amber I've ever seen. And I bought this necklace. It's beautiful.

ANN
Bootiful.

TYLEA
The workmanship. I bought it as the events were going on. I thought, these are my worry beads; so every time I wear it, it's a calming thing because I bought it on 9/11.

ANN
[mimics her] I bought it on 9/11.

TYLEA
I can't imagine the hours, the crafting that went into it.

ANN
She repeating what the saleslady told her. The buy this, buy that Mumbo Jumbo.

TYLEA
And the boxes, I save all the boxes. They remind me of the joy of the purchase. I haven't even worn it anywhere. I guess that's when you know you've made it on some level. You have it and you don't flaunt it.

ANN
Those police in Walnut Creek pulled out their wallets and gave An three $20 bills. Sixty dollars to get outta Dodge, oh, they never gave those Southern black boys a dime to catch the next train running. It was get out before the sun rises or … An don't mind going back to Berkeley. Berkeley the only place in the universe where white folk smile at you and nod, the way colored do down South. Of course, these white folk high or butt naked. Old hippies. An don't mind.

TYLEA
Whatever I talk about, she talks about. Maybe she admires me.

ANN
Some people stuck on stupid, some people stuck on theyself. An like to think about world events. If the World Trade had happened in Harlem, this would be a different world: [into a microphone, in a newscaster's voice] "A plane driven by brown men landed in the middle of the Harlem State Office Building, killing hundreds of Harlemites. And, oh my god, missing Bill Clinton by a matter of yards." [drops mike] The fire engines would be late as usual. Who gets to ghetto fires on time?

TYLEA
So did you hear all the cursing on network TV? The fireman who saw the first plane hit said, HOLY SHIT. And the TV stations played that over and over. HOLY SHIT HOLY SHIT so that's it? We can curse on network TV now? What happened to the FCC's seven forbidden words that made George Carlin? Who cares? Holy shit? The first night David Letterman was back and talking about the attack, he said, the GODDAMN terrorists…

ANN
An trying to figure out why this didn't happen before. Like when Kennedy was killed. [on the mike] OH SHIT. SOMEBODY KILLED THE PRESIDENT. DAMN. WHAT HAPPENED? WHO FUCKED UP? Or like down South on the news when Martin Luther King was killed, can you hear it in real life? "Martin Luther Coon was killed. Good. Who took that nigger out?"

TYLEA
There she goes with the n word again. ANN
Nigguz I know said they were watching the world trade to see if nigguz was jumping out the windows. And you really couldn't tell. And that made folks nervous cuz how you know what to feel if you can't figure out they color.

ANN
So now we're just war-crazed.

TYLEA
Bomb the terrorists.

ANN
McDonnell Douglas.

TYLEA
The jump-jet.

ANN
More F-15s.

TYLEA
Get the War Machine ready.

ANN
Don't forget they're here.

TYLEA
How you gonna bomb Jersey City?

ANN
You might hit the Sopranos.

TYLEA
How you gonna bomb Oakland,

ANN
An island of eighty dialects?

TYLEA
How you gonna bomb Florida?

ANN
A foreign country inside a foreign country?

TYLEA
We are a foreign country

ANN
Africans Asians Europeans

ANN
Squatting on

Counter-Terrorism: An abridged version

ANN & TYLEA
Cherokee Seminole soil.

ANN & TYLEA
You gonna bomb Trenton?

ANN
Passaic?

TYLEA
Camden?

ANN
Newark?

TYLEA
Just take out New Jersey, right?

ANN
Can you smart-bomb Boston and bypass Cambridge?

TYLEA
Dearborn and not hit the Grosse Pointes?

ANN
Fremont, California?

TYLEA
Oops, we nuked Silicon Valley.

ANN
Can we make a smart-bomb with a racial profiling chip?

TYLEA
Technology's a bitch, ain't he?
An still scared of white people cuz they invented Godzilla. Racism like Godzilla. Just when you think it's gone for good – and An don't believe in race -

TYLEA
No one cares about race when they need a kidney
– But racism, it's our own personal Godzilla.

ANN
And it never goes for good. Just a sleeping in the San Francisco Bay right near the Ferry Bldg. Go watch the movie. You'll see.

END PLAY

"Wait Just A Goddam Minute"

A Fat Drama in the Space of a Working Lunch

Characters

ANNIE AND NEDRA, TWO BLACK WOMEN BUILT FOR THE LONG HAUL, BOTH OF WHOM ARE WRITERS

ALSO: A PARADE OF BLACK WOMEN, BUXOM, STYLISH. CAN BE A CINEMATIC FILM AS A BACKDROP.

Setting

TWO CHAIRS AND A TABLE AT AN OUTDOOR RESTAURANT.

#73NEVERGIVEUP#
I went to this fat lady's store to buy a slip. Only I wasn't big enough.

NEDRA
Back to Macy's basement.

ANNIE
But while I was there, there were all these fat ladies and I swear each one had a man waiting in the aisle, in the parking lot, looking just as pleased to be stuck there with his old lady as the guys in the marmy swarmy size 4-8 guccipuccis.

NEDRA
I don't understand why you were surprised.

ANNIE
Well, there I was in the middle of this fattie store in the middle of this fatty stereotype in the middle of buying that fat is not sexual.

NEDRA
Humph.

ANNIE
And I said to myself out loud right there in the aisle with the size 46 to 52 black lace slips and teddies hanging there.

NEDRA
Silkily hanging there, weren't they?

ANNIE
I mean. Looking at me and my big butt but not big enough hips, and I said, WAIT JUST A GODDAM MINUTE.

NEDRA
But that was a couple of years ago.

ANNIE
So it's taken a while to register. But I've finally started having fantasies. Can you believe it, nude and running in the forest: tits for days, buns bouncing, thighs to here and loving it, getting off on it.

NEDRA
I'm having the avocado salad. I have to lose 30 pounds.

ANNIE
I'm getting a cheeseburger. Take heart. Someone said psychics need weight so they won't float off the astral plane and lose their way back.

NEDRA
We didn't order drinks yet, Annie. Flotation level is ground to honeybuns. [They begin talking over each other, each musing yet listening to the other, akin to undressing in front of each other.]

ANNIE
I've always had these short friends, 5'2, 5'; my mother's a little woman. Mouths to go. You know when you're larger you tend to try to package what you say. But little women, do they give a fuck?

NEDRA
But the kind of guy I fantasize about being with when I'm slim is this cruel kind of sadistic humper-dumper who gets his and gets off.... and my husband is so different from that. I know even if I were out there, that kind of GQ guy I would never go for. But your mind works those possibilities. You know?

ANNIE
I was thinking about promoting my next book and I really figured I didn't want to look, on the jacket, like a mammy, you know, fat and black.

NEDRA
Actually, sex is different when my weight is up. I lose – uh something. Control.

ANNIE
Then I thought: Oh, wait, a goddam minute. I'm not the pedagogic tit. Wait just …did I hear you say "you lose something?" Back up. [A bell signals their orders are ready. As they get up to get them, a parade of stylish, black, fat women, alone, in tandem, some escorted, beaming, sexy, happy, passes by, from one end of the stage to another. For a few minutes, they get lost in the women, first like a crazy kind of conga line and then like pedestrians crossing the street in two directions. They sit down with their food. They resume talking and eat, sharing small portions of each other's plate]

NEDRA
Yeah, you know, you lose yourself. You get lost in it. When I'm fat, I mean fat, we go at it, like pigs wallowing in slop.

ANNIE
You are believable. I can see it right now.

NEDRA
Let the rolls roll. No holding back. No holding your stomach in, lots of grunting and laughing and spitting and shaking and whooping.

ANNIE
More cushion for the pushing.

NEDRA
Then I lose my weight and I become different. Straight humping. Serious in-out business.

ANNIE
A sex object?

NEDRA
No big funsies but I can get in all of my old clothes. So what's this pedagogic tit?

ANNIE
We saw this famous black woman writer and it was like she was being worshipped. Her every word was a transmogrification.

NEDRA
What is that?

ANNIE
Her audience was practically milking her tit. It was just heavy duty, no fooling around. You are there to save people's souls in the space of an hour, and you're not even a believer in God.

ANNIE
When my son's orthodontist found out I write poetry, he went into ecstasy over Maya Angelou, and said her malocclusion just accentuated her authority. I mean, give mammy a break. Can she rest in the unreconstructed peace of the 19th century?

NEDRA
Some folks never get enough.

ANNIE
I mean, what else do they want? They have the jobs, the money, the nuclear-that's-it-folks, and still they want to suck at the tit?

NEDRA
It's the Saint Mammy Syndrome. My girl friend Rasagha has this baby who is old enough to walk up to her, unbutton her blouse, and pull the tit out of the bra, and go at it like it's a chocolate Popsicle. Your own baby is one thing, but a whole nation. Give it up.

ANNIE
And I have this friend, skinny and white as a picket fence, and we were driving through town, and this big black woman crosses in front of his car, his little white Vega, and he said, with a sigh if you please, "Why are black women so big?" And I swear I said, "So they won't get run over by skinny mf's in compact cars."

NEDRA
Well, the fat fantasy says a lot. I used to dream that I was this skinny, teardrop-waist woman, always getting raped in a high rise office building by the bosses' sons– there are a few of them– and the window washers stood there on those swings outside of the 80th floor with their mouths wide open.

ANNIE
Were the window washers black?

NEDRA
Did you have to ask?

ANNIE
Oh, that was fucked.

NEDRA
I know, but just at that point, it did it. Always. For a long time.

ANNIE
Even after you got married?

NEDRA
A long, long time.

ANNIE
Isn't that kind of common for women though?

NEDRA
Common, my ass. They were a product of my imagination and my complexes.

ANNIE
Tell me if I'm lying, I'm flying. Haven't we seen, in the space of the time we've been here, at least five humongous women walk by, each one looking like a million dollars, and wif a man on her arm?!!

NEDRA
Wif? Wif a man on her arm? Wif?

ANNIE
Yeah, wif, as in can you get a whiff uh dis?

NEDRA
Dis?

ANNIE
Yeah, you know, like a diss jockey. You and me, hon, we're working it through.

NEDRA
It's hard work, you got that much right.

ANNIE
It's probably going to get harder the further away from the old fantasies we get.

NEDRA
I still get them, but they come in like a distorted picture on an old TV. And I'm just about ready to stop trying to tune em in.

ANNIE
It's probably just a rerun. Let's figure out the tip.

NEDRA
What about the book jacket?

ANNIE
Why don't we just pose nude and flopping back-to-back, buns on tops of buns, hot mama burgers?

NEDRA
Now that would sell.

ANNIE
There'd be closet doors banging down.
NEDRA
But would they read it?

ANNIE
Who's talking books? I'm going for the million-selling poster: Fat Women at Lunch.

NEDRA
What if someone offered you megabucks? Seriously.

ANNIE
Seriously, let's pay the tab and get back to work

END PLAY

A Moment of Silence

A Moment of Silence

Characters

REGINA, A REGISTERED NURSE [RN], BLACK, ABOUT 40 YEARS OLD, OLDER THAN HER YEARS

DR. REMINGTON, ABOUT 55, NONBLACK, HEAD OF AN EXPERIMENTAL UNIT AT THE INFANT & CHILDREN'S HOSPITAL[INCH]

KATYDID, REGINA'S YOUNGER SISTER

2 HIP HOPPERS

2 MEDS

CHARLES FREE, REGINA'S DEAD SON, PERENNIALLY 17

CHARLETTA AND ABYSINTHE, REGINA'S FELLOW NURSES

ADMIN. ASST.

BABYMOMMA

[Regina & DR. REMINGTON ington go up to an incubator in the back of the stage. DR. REMINGTON ington moves away from Regina as she approaches it. She peers in]

DR. REM
I'd like to think you've seen a little bit of everything, Regina.

REGINA
Some people think working 8th floor INCH anesthetizes you.

DR. REM
You need to brace yourself.

REGINA
Rem, I've seen so many little sweet ones go cold and blue. [A yellow-lime blurry light shaft like a supernatural glow emanates from the incubator. Regina steps back as if jolted by electricity.] He can't even scream. That's a tittle [the sound of other babies crying, down the hall, is muffled, piped in from a monitor]. It's more like a gasp for life and air and wonder than an actual scream.

DR. REMINGTON
Touch it, Regina.

REGINA
[bending over the incubator] It? This is a male.

DR. REMINGTON
[Steps back, reads into his micro tape recorder.] Regina Arterberry, my subject nurse, is talking to it, cooing, actually. She's seeing it for the first time, I for the second. I could hardly bear to look before. So so strange a configuration. It has a baby's puckered pink face with a protuberance where its mouth out to... is supposed to... where a normal human's mouth should be. Instead there's a hard waxy yellow protuberance like the yellow of a sunflower, like the hardness of gold, like a set of wax lips. [He stops, clicks off the recorder, looks at Regina, goes over to her back.] This is not flustering you?

REGINA
He's alive. He's making eye contact.

DR. REM
They destroyed them in Chernobyl as soon as they were born. Hideous mutations of the human form.

REGINA
What are they thinking to do here?

DR. REM
Look at its eyes.

REGINA
The pupil fills the whole surface. And no lashes. [Regina begins to weep then stops herself.] I can't turn away from a life.

DR. REM
[talking into his recorder] Its hair is straight, black and sticks up in clumps like weeds in a marsh. Its pupils are like those of an animal. Its torso is round, ball-like, not oblong like an infant's. It's covered with soft yellow fuzz, like dyed blonde hair on a peach, as if peroxide had been poured into the amniotic fluid.... Look at the feet, Regina.

REGINA
[avoids doing that; goes to get droppers and begins to feed it.] His legs are spindly.

DR. REM
[directs her to its feet while recording] Its feet are webbed like duck feet and the same color as the waxy mouth.

REGINA
He won't take any nourishment.

DR. REM
Regina, look at his feet.

REGINA
[She uncovers the blanket, and is so startled she drops it on the floor] What is it, DR. REMINGTON ?

DR. REM
What does it look like?

REGINA
Like a duckling with part of a child's face and part of its body.

DR. REM
That's what it is.

REGINA
But how could it be?
[Back on the floor. The strange gold light can be seen in the background. Two medical types in uniform are standing up in the bare spotlight. One is eating Chinese food with a fork out of a white foam dinner container. The other is sorting through the contaminated waste looking for something.]

1ST MED
Don't get shit on my food, now.

2ND MED
Don't worry.

1ST MED
Seen Dr Strangelove today?

2ND MED
He was acting like nothing's going on.

1ST MED
I saw him talking shit, like mutation, species, droplets, cellular plant.

2ND MED
He probably said "cellular implant." That's his job [pulls stethoscope out of his top, keeps looking, spills clothes onto the floor, finally finds a needle, pockets it, and keeps looking.]

1ST MED
Everybody knows. Why do they think it's a secret? Somebody posted a name for it over the microwave: the infant death mortality squad.

2ND MED
Redundant. It's called the mutation project, the Infant Children's Hospital Mutation Experimental Site.

1ST MED
It's unreal like some shit in the movies, Weird. I call him Dr Weirdo. Dr go-get-em weirdo.
[Spotlight shifts to the sign outside the hospital. Sign reads INCH. Three hip hop types, baggy jeans, backward caps, heavy sweatshirt-type jacket, are dragging a body [can be big dummy body's, similarly dressed] up to the hospital entrance and leaving it there running off stage. This action is a ballet, fluid moving from hip hoppers to the meds. Gunfire. Rockets & mortar fire going off seemingly but turn out to be cars/freeway traffic.

HIP HOPPERS
Is Charles dead? Is he dead??? I don't know…What the fu..? Get him down there… He's too old for this place. INCH for kids… Hurry up, mafucker. This is a children's and babies center…What the fuck? Damn, Charles heavy. Is he breathing? Is he dead? I don't know…Hurry up! [They rush off stage. Sound of car door fades. Sounds of cars passing by. Hospital personnel rush out. A Dr., a nurse, a security guard & an orderly with a stretcher. They start examining him in haste.]

MEDS
Does he have a pulse? Get him on the stretcher! Hurry up, will you? Is he breathing? He's.... [They rush him off. A moment of silence.]

DR. REM
[comes out looks at cars going by]... Jesus Christ, what a waste! [Lights go out. Come up on DR. REMINGTON & Regina again.]

DR. REM
If necessity is the mother of invention, then sometimes science is the mother of the invention.

REGINA
It's male.

DR. REMINGTON
It's a male of its species. It couldn't have survived otherwise.

REGINA
I've been calling him Charlie.

DR. REMINGTON
I know. I've heard you. That was your son's name, wasn't it?

REGINA
He was Charles. I keep expecting him to say something or to make a sound. I know by his eyes he can hear well. Why can't he do anything but gurgle?

DR. REMINGTON
He doesn't appear to have the vocal cords of either a duck or a human.

REGINA
[to the crib.]White coats, white walls, white silences. I for one love your gold. You bring back gold in the morning, Charlie Quick Gold in the morn. The turn in the road, Charlie Quack. [Regina walks over to the crib and starts singing softly, "Charlie Quick Quack, quick quack, Charlie quit that.]

DR. REMINGTON
[leaves the room but not the stage, shaking his head; Katydid enters. They skirt each other.] Regina's is utterly trustworthy. I would trust her with my life.

KATYDID
My sister has no life. [in background, Regina sweeps & mops the area around the crib with incredible joy]

DR. REMINGTON
She's bonded with it, become its caretaker.

KATYDID
Before all this, Gina's flat over on 44th was too close to INCH. She couldn't bear to be here after my nephew was killed. She wanted to move farther away. Now it's not close enough. She walks the mile in 15 minutes.
[Lights goes off Rem, Katydid, and onto the hip hoppers and corpse.. The sign glows again. The corpse tries to move in fits and starts, but can't make it off the ground. The hip-hops pull his pants off. The med doctors pull his shirt and cap off. Lights goes on DR. REMINGTON and Katydid at opposite end off stage. They speak in direction of audience not facing each other. Theirs is a dance of seduction-rejection]

DR. REMINGTON
Katydid. Is that your given name?

KATYDID
Katy. Then because I was always getting into trouble, the others got to saying, Katy did it. So it stuck.

DR. REMINGTON
One Katydid in a sea of Rashondas and Tanikwas.

KATYDID
You got your generations mixed up. I was with the Denises, Andreas and Joyces.

DR. REM
You know the Katydid's a grasshopper?

KATYDID
Whichever way you're heading, don't even go there.
[Black out.]

REGINA
[Regina comes on stage pulling on the straps of a bathing suit, and then putting her hair into a swimming cap. She starts to pull on a pair of flippers but has a time bending down.] Oh Charlie, we've got to get you in our pool. I've got to touch my toes so I can get you in the pool for a splash around. [She gets in a shallow wading pool at upstage, lots of splashing. She's laughing. There is obviously another with her, gurgling and cooing. You can hear them having a good time. Down stage 2 nurses walk by very slowly so they can peep at the pool scene].

CHARLETTA
She eats all her meals at INCH & works 14-day shifts.

ABYSINTHE
[goes closer to Regina] It's crazy, but I just want to see it. [water splashes on her. She wipes it off with disgust] Charletta, I just want to know– is it black or is it white?

CHARLETTA
Regina worked herself to death after the boy died. I think working here on this floor, one floor above where they had brought Charlie Free, working like a nigger in the field day and night, night and day and your baby is DOA literally one floor beneath your aching feet. And they're picking at his little organs one-by-one like crows. 'Oh, look his liver wasn't shot. Let's pick that sucker out. And his eyes. Oh, this young buck has 20/20. Whoever gets these won't even need laporoscopy. And check the kidneys, check the kidneys. Get everything. Just get everything. Gut him...' And there's Reggie taking temps and writing orders like a good RN.. Yeah, yeah, yeah. It's a wonder she didn't die right then. They'll never take out my stuff, none. Oh no, let this body go back into the muddy mud with everything it had when the breath left. Abysinthe, you can be a

donor if you want to be.

ABYSINTHE
[looking at Regina splashing & whooping all the while]. She's enjoying herself.
[Lights fade. Splashing noises on. First Regina's silhouette can be seen & then flippers which look like duck feet.]
[Black out.]

DR. REMINGTON
[DR. REMINGTON is talking to an admin. assistant who takes notes] She's black, a single mother.

ADMIN. ASST.
Uh huh.

DR. REMINGTON
He was born when she was 16, died when he was 17 in a gang shoot-out.
Admin. Asst.
With all due respect, what does this have to do with the experiment?

DR. REMINGTON
History will want to know this. Think of Oppenheimer.
Lights Fade.

KATYDID
[Katydid comes back out with a dinner wrapped in tin foil.] Regina, I got your dinner..[Looks around] Probably giving him a bubble bath... [walks to the other side of the stage. DR. REMINGTON comes back sees her, turns his back to her. Looks at her to see if she's looking at him, She unfolds the aluminum foil.] You ever had sweet potato pie, DR. REMINGTON ?

DR. REMINGTON
Can't say I have. Pumpkin, yes, at the holiday.

KATYDID
Regina taught me how to make it. Even down to picking the yams. Long ones make the best... I'll just leave it here,. a piece for you inside Regina's dinner.
[Lights go out]
[DR. REMINGTON says, "Thank you tremendously!" She says, "It's just a piece of pie."]

KATYDID
[As Katydid talks, the gold light starts to get brighter, then blinking bright and it stays that way until she shades her eyes; then it fades away] I'm worried about Regina. I don't know if she's paying her rent on time. Her landlord is the nicest person in the world. But gratitude turns on a dime. [She folds up the aluminum foil. It's crazy to be up in here. Up in here. You couldn't pay me to work here. Always on call, on duty working her tail off. Devoting her entire life to INCH. Why? What for? Story of her life. Work, work, work, work, work, work. She's gonna work so hard she loses her mind? And the next thing you know she's homeless. I hate the homeless especially when they're black. That's a modern redundancy. We've been homeless for 400 years. [She turns to the admin. asst. who writes mechanically] Six months ago, I took my unemployment and gave them a bullshit story about getting a job in New York City. If I was out of work, why not see the world while I'm at it. And I learned about black people being homeless. I'm walking from the "Y" to the half-price ticket booth to see CATS, Times Square with all the tourists and garment factory workers and the homeless who, I'd like to say, in New York City have a NIMBY attitude. The homeless here are so passive they're actually begging. They have the pleading posture. They work on empathy here. That don't play in New York. They have the managerial homeless in Manhattan. Mental but they're managing it, they know how and when to go crazy. How and when to get in your face. "I may not know Karate but I know Ka-razy." Being homeless in New York is about real estate, baby. Location, Location, Location. Here they position themselves on the edge of the corner as if to say, I'm on the edge…Help me!! I'm falling. In New York, they're in the middle of the sidewalk. I was going to a Knicks game at Madison Square Garden. Do you think this guy could have rolled himself up

so I wouldn't have to step over him? Puh!! I don't think so. They occupy their turf and you're just an invader. "Gimme some money bitch….I know you got some money…Gimme some…Well get on out of here, black bitch." They have so much energy. They work the streets. Here, I've seen this same guy- blond scruffy hair, in fatigues for 3 years, on the corner near the freeway. Same sign: Will work for food Same silent plea. Same edge. Bro, if you were going over the edge you would have gone. But my biggest fright was outside Andronico's, you know your quasi-upscale scones/4 for $6 Berkeley supermarket. A black woman like me, a brown skinned doppelganger, very school teacherish, dressed ok, looking like my kind, you know how you pass somebody on the street you think "we're the same station in life" and she approached me. Can you give me some money? I know you can make a living like that. They can make $50 even more a day if they persist. But I was thinking: What if I end up like her? I'm good with signs. But what am I going to do? Be like the New Yorkers or the ones here?[Spotlight goes on nurses]

CHARLETTTA
Where'd that name? Charlie?

ABYSINTHE
I think she got it from Peanuts.

CHARLETTTA
Penis??

ABYSINTHE
No, Peanuts the comic strip with Lucy. Cuz I heard Dr. Rem talking bout Charlie was right up next to Lucy in the evolutionary train. So Lucy's what drove Charlie Brown nuts. So, I'm thinking that's where she got Charlie from.

CHARLETTTA
[They start bringing in baby stuff- stroller, Pampers] She's gonna need these if she has a baby.

ABYSINTHE
She's not having a baby. It's already here.

CHARLETTA
Really? This is my contribution. I don't baby-sit, I don't want to watch these babies. But she need Pampers.

ABYSINTHE
She's not having a baby.

CHARLETTA
Who baby is she having?

ABYSINTHE
She never got pregnant.

CHARLETTA
Who's the baby daddy?

ABYSINTHE
Science of Technology.

CHARLETTA
I don't care who the babydaddy is. Here some baby stuff cuz these babydaddies out here they got all of nothing to give these babies.

ABYSINTHE
She is a grown ass woman. She is not having no baby.

ABYSINTHE
Then why is she acting like a brandnew mother?

CHARLETTTA
[Says this last to the back where Regina is] Don't be the sister from another planet now. You can be the brother from another planet and still get you a white girl. But if you're the sister from another planet-oh, no you just gonna be a bag lady. Out there homeless, lost in space. You can do bad by yourself. You can do bad by yo'self. But you can't do bad all by yo'self. You need to check in periodically, sister. [Katydid comes on, the spotlight shifts to her]

KATYDID
You never heard of that:: you can do bad by yo'self? That's 'The Black Woman's National Anthem.' Don't let no man drag you down. You can do bad by yo'self. You ain't a white woman. You ain't helpless. You got struggle in the genes. Get up. If you fall down 125 times, get up 125 times. Don't let no man use you for a piss pot. You can do bad by yo'self.
[Stage darkens and then the hip hoppers talk over & at each other at Charles Free's gravestone.]

HIP HOPPER #1
We RAW PRODUCT. Das our name, dig? RAW PRODUCT. That's who we are & what we are.

HIP HOPPER #2
Yeah, went to get a burrito in Berkeley and next door the white boys were playing John Coltrane, no, a John Coltrane score. Hah! Sheet music. Shit!! Music is my blood but if I never took a lesson held a clarinet tuba violin flute snared a drum bruised a thumb playing on a trumpet trying to be Dizzy Gillespie I gotta watch? Watch, ma' fucker, no I ain't gotta watch nothing I'm a player.

HIP HOPPER #1
I ain't dead. I know niggas was fabulous raw product for the last 400 years and capitalism functions high white and mighty off RAW PRODUCT. Capitalism say, we got to commodify John Coltrane. Put his shit down on paper, sell it, buy it, store it, CD it and then we don't need no John. Die, motherfuckers, for all we care. We will put on our stone edifices. SMOOTH JAZZ and on yours NIGGERS WATCHED AND SLAVED AND FORGOT THEY DREAMS.
[Flirting outrageously, moving toward each other from opposite stages of the stage & then away, DR. REMINGTON & Katydid each sip coffee from Styrofoam cups, oblivious to the hip hoppers]

HIP HOPPER #2
[Lights fade on the hip hoppers but the voice is loud, punctuated with hip hop body language] Go eat a burrito, mafucker, with hi tech no sauce, we are RAW PRODUCT that can't be commodified because we're free even if some of us only get freed by making death our creed.

DR. REMINGTON
You're an American!

KATYDID
I'm a Black Woman!

DR. REMINGTON
You're an American! You don't want to face it. You want to call yourself all these appellations; black, African-American, Nubian, but you're an American. You know how you can find out how American you are? Try going with an African. Try it. Do it.

KATYDID
No can do. 1st thing; can't he do something with his hair? Curl it or twist it or dread it?

DR. REMINGTON
You're an American not the kind with the flag in front of your house and a picture of your grandfather waving goodbye to your grandmother from the USS Torpedo. Not that kind. You're an American. You make $28,000 a year and you're a whiz because you have 3 colors TV's in your 2 bedroom apt., you leased a Lexus.

KATYDID
And a Beamer and a Geo all in the last 3 years.

DR. REMINGTON
You have a cell phone and a pager.

KATYDID
And the phone's been turned off twice in the last 6 months.

DR. REMINGTON
And you're about to find out just how American you are.

KATYDID
I'm not into white men. Forget it I don't care how much money you have or how sweet your Beamer is.

DR. REMINGTON
Because you're going to try it with an African?

KATYDID
Even if he wears orange pants. That's all right. He can wear him some orange pants if he wants to. If it feels good, it's all right.

DR. REMINGTON
So you two snuggle up, black on black, oh how special.

KATYDID
The first thing I found out about my African is he's not African. "I'm Ibo."

DR. REMINGTON
Africa is a continent, sweetheart, not a country.

KATYDID
That's exactly what he said. All men are alike.

DR. REMINGTON
So there you are with your...

KATYDID
With my Nigerian honey and it's Saturday night and he's going to Amole's Dance club to see his fellows cuz he got that African unity in his blood just like we got disunity in the blood. And there I go, getting ready to step out with sisterfriends and boy friend says, "And where are you going, my lovely tulip
– cut it, You're going with your homies. I'm not sitting here staring at the wall.

– I want to know what time you'll be back here

– I do not need a daddy!

– That's not what you said last night. 'Oh daddy, I need you, daddy."

And some nights I can get with the program and stay home and then that one night when I can't, somehow we get to scuffling. And the next thing I know somebody's saying 'fuck you, your mamma, your friends, Africa, Nigeria, whatever. Fuck it."

DR. REMINGTON
And you revert back to basics and say:

KATYDID
Get out!

DR. REMINGTON
And he said:

KATYDID
'No you get out. This is my house.' And I said your house? You don't even have a green card. And it's all over.

DR. REMINGTON
Your wonderful relationship with your wonderful African because you're a not all that wonderful American. Salute that flag. Is that a wig you're wearing?

KATYDID
No, I'm the Queen of Sheba reincarnated. Yes, it's a wig and I like it down to my butt. Now![they fade into shadows]
[These characters, babymomma, Charles, and a hip hopper, inhabit the stage, frantic, yet thoroughly unaware of each other]

BABY MOMMA
I had his baby he my baby daddy. My babydaddy momma crazy. What am I supposed to do? My baby daddy's dead. You hear me, dead. I gotta get paid I don't care about what she said a play baby shit maybe it is a play baby what is she playing with? Maybe I need a play baby too. Somepin someone else feed shelter and buy new clothes for.

HIP HOPPER #1
Get hi' gold toof git his gode toof.. too late dang... They got him. Shit, couda got a gold toof.

BABY MOMMA
[shuffles papers] Why cain't I get social security? He didn't make no money? He made hecka money. Mo' money than you ever made.[throws papers down]

CHARLES FREE
I gotta leave some babies, gotta plant some seeds. If I'm outta here before thirty, I gotta do the duty hit some booty plant a little bit of me in some little cutie.[spins and spins] Where are the Characters? The Characters [looks around for them] They should have been here by now. they go from weddings to funerals to baby showers to graduations to garage sales to protest meetings to sr centers. Martin Luther King's Day to wherever you need some they'll bring you the whole shebang just put it in the paper and they'll be there in whatever color dress and suit you need they performing community service a thousand points of lights street corner-to-street corner resuscitation my momma do it says it beats soap operas it caint be all bad.
[Spot light goes off Charles Free, onto Katydid first, then DR. REMINGTON, the nurses walking by]

KATYDID
I'm worried about Regina not coming home anymore. My room is my space, separate and apart from society.

DR. REMINGTON
Maybe she's merged into and is one with society.

KATYDID
{Flirtatiously] When you share space with a person... You can't be alone. You have to use both your conscience and your unconscious at the same time.

CHARLETTA
[walking by with Abysinthe. Spotlight goes on them] She's trying to train him like a dawg. But he ain't black. He ain't used to being whipped and then pussy whipped too.

ABYSINTHE
He's a pet. No hang-ups, no expectations, no ill will, no grudges. No let down.

CHARLETTA
Well, at least it's not a donkey. We got enough jackasses running around here without making one up in a test tube.

[they walk off stage. Spotlight goes on Katydid and DR. REMINGTON.]

DR. REM
[Flirting back with her] Katydid, I didn't know you were a student of psychology.

KATYDID
Sharing space means one person has to reduce the stress by bearing the burden intermittently... that's why people pick partners with similar backgrounds. Because culture consists of unconscious habitual behavior.

DR. REM
Can you give me examples? Can you be specific? Concrete. Come closer. I don't bite.

CHARLETTA
[Spot light goes off Dr & Katydid and onto nurse] This woman named Marietta come in here and didn't find out until she was a good 60, 65, she had a gall bladder problem. They went in and found out her stomach was reversed. It had been inside her backwards all the time.

ABYSINTHE
Like what?

CHARLETTA
Over there when it should have been over here.

ABYSINTHE
So what's that got to do with this? [points to glow]

CHARLETTA
It means nature, Mother Nature, isn't perfect.

ABYSINTHE
She fucked up and produced a duck?

CHARLETTA
Let's just say it's adaptation. It goes on all the time. Being black isn't where we started, but here we are, high blood and all. [lights off them, back on Katydid]

KATYDID
Closer, huh? One small step for man one giant step for mankind?

DR. REM
A small step for you. A giant step for everybody.

KATYDID
[starts getting as busy and nervous and frantic as babymomma was} You can't get in trouble feeding people. And then sometimes you have to go to the trouble of doing it, just cook it because... you need it. Regina likes my cooking. Now you know Regina never asked for chittlins until now, until Charlie Quick Quack. They have chittlins at this place, you would go and get them. The Down Home Cafe. But you can only get them on Fridays like the Catholics eat fish on Fridays. But you can't get anybody to clean chittlins anymore. Who wants to clean shit out of a hog's bowels. The house not just the kitchen, stinks. So you get to Down Home on Fridays and if you have to go after work, they say: ain't no chitlins left, you have to call in advance, way in advance to reserve your chitlins. And so you call. You call and you call and you call, and they don't even have call waiting. It's busy all the time

DR. REM
What's that smell?

KATYDID
Chitlins. For Regina. From the Chinese.

DR. REM
You mean you're carrying around chitterlings from Chinatown.

KATYDID
For my sister, yes. Chinatown, no. If I can ever get them to answer the phone at the black restaurant, I'd get them there. They don't answer their phone. Here I am trying to buy black and I can't order

the chittlins. So way cross-town they have this place called The Kitchen next door to a hotel with a Chinese restaurant next door and a black restaurant in it. The hotel closed and the Chinese just took to cooking the menu from the hotel restaurant and I have to say I admire them. I mean they come here, don't know tit from tat and they roll up their sleeves and do the best they can and they don't mind cleaning those chittlins EVERYDAY OF THE WEEK. Humph. And that's where I go to get Regina's chitlins, way cross town to the Chinese. If the Korean can straighten hair and braid it and the Chinese make chitlins that taste like down home, maybe it's time for us to do something different too. Break out, be unbelievable.

DR. REM
One small step for man, a grand step for mankind.[He leaves the stage, Katydid gives the food to Regina who picks over it; as Regina talks, Katydid eats bit-by-bit]

REGINA
That Charlie talks in a duck's voice, kind of like Donald Duck. But when he gets excited, it all sounds like quacking. Then it seems I'm the only one who can understand him. [She goes off stage. DR. REMINGTON comes back]

DR. REM
Miss Katydid, you are an important component of this... operation.

KATYDID
She needs to eat. I don't care how nutty things get.

DR. REMINGTON
Yes, she does appear to be getting her appetite back... would you like to know how Charlie was conceived?

KATYDID
No, I don't care for horror movies.

DR. REM
This concerns you. It was a discarded embryo and I guess you could say science gone amuck.

KATYDID
Why are you telling me? Isn't this confidential?

DR. REM
Yes, it's top secret. Like the Atom Bomb, the Manhattan Project.

KATYDID
I am the wrongest person in the whole world to know secrets. I'm a mouth. That's my true occupation, running my mouth.

DR. REM
I want you to tell people about this [he gestures around]

KATYDID
Gossip?

DR. REM
Spread the rumors far and wide. Like the CIA buying guns and drugs for the gangs in LA.

KATYDID
Hold up. That was the truth.

DR. REM
Many people think not.

KATYDID
[He begins walking offstage and she begins to have to shout at his back] You want the truth to sound like a big fat lie?
[FAST Fade. Shadows emerge. A sign says: THE BALLET OF THE ORGAN DONOR. The hip hoppers begin pulling off Free's pants. Money, change, credit cards fall from his body, glow in the dark. $$ signs float around the stage. The lyrics of the song "Money, money, money," can be heard and others. "Your love gives me such a thrill, but your love don't pay my bill. I need money." The Hip hops are caught between the desire to spend– they grab at the $$ signs but can't secure them so they go back to the body and the passion to rape the body of all that is viable, clearly getting off; it's orgasmic. The string of credit cards, incredible in length, occupies them, trying to fold it up and put it in their wallet. It's

A Moment of Silence

impossible to do. The meds in medical greens and whites, docs with stethoscopes, meds with ice buckets of all sizes, a person with a Jaws of life-type outsize pliers come from opposite side of the stage. They begin orgiastic exclamation and swoons as they pull out a kidney, the heart, his heart still beating [the sound of it stops all momentarily]– then they say in unity "Brain Dead" and resume their respective pillaging of the body. When they all finish, there is nothing to do nothing left. The light shows them leaving & washes over and over the emptied area where the body was. Only Free's cap remains.]
[Black Out. Lights come up on Katydid, and Charletta]

KATYDID
How big is he? About yea big [motions with her hand]

CHARLETTA
Have you seen it? To know for sure.

KATYDID
Rem, are you calling my sister crazy?

REGINA
[Regina comes onstage with a TV-VCR] I know people are talking about me. But I know he has feelings, Katy.

KATYDID
I've heard the quacking, Regina but it sounds like a duck to me. Maybe I'm the crazy one– a duck in a hospital. When I go by and make my talk to it like he's a fellow– how ya doing?- it quacks like it can hear me.

REGINA
If you can understand that he can hear you, that he has perceptions, why can't you listen to him? You listen to your dog. You listen to your cat, why not Charlie Quick Quack? [Regina sets up her TV-VCR as Dr. Rem comes onstage and start talking to Katydid]

KATYDID
Are the pro-life gonna start protesting here?

DR. REM
Why would they? They don't know about it yet. They kept Dolly a secret until she was seven months old.

KATYDID
But when they find out?

DR. REM
Actually, they consider cloning cells from the embryo- stem cells- the violation of the life principle. Scientists put together a monkey with a jelly fish. [The ballet music resumes and Charles Free's voice, a disembodied sound]

CHARLES
Grieve Motherfuckers, Grieve mafucker. Pour your heart out and grieve for your mother. The heart the head nigger in charge needs a break. A moment of refusal for the cruel. So grieve mufucker grieve before you leave this scene of the crime so when you get ready to step out of life some other mafuckers will pour out their heart and grieve motherfucker grieve motherfucker. Pour your heart out & grieve for your brothers.

KATYDID
This ain't a monkey and a jelly fish. And where did the monkey's dick get into the jellyfish?? Answer that one. You can't. But how did you all get a cross between a baby and a duck; that's all I want to know.

DR. REMINGTON
The most important thing is for this not to get on television or into the news. That would be death by sensationalism to the project.

KATYDID
I saw Malcolm X's daughter Attalla Shabazz, Farrakhan and Mike Wallace on "60 minutes." It was all arranged and edited down from 4 hours of interviewing. I know some shit was flying there. She lost her mother behind that shit. And the TV thinks they can show me one piece of the puzzle. Recycled. All of TV is recycled now anyway. Why do we even have to pay for TV's? They should just be like park benches. FREE. Public Shit. That's all it is– very

public shit, 24-7. Anybody think newscasters know more than kindergarten teachers? They should just switch positions. "Now boys & girls at 6 am today, a man was shot to death in South San Francisco. And over at the Oakland Zoo a cub was born." Oh, how's this for realism? 'White women who love to fuck, love to talk about fucking, are obsessed with dick size & don't go out with black guys in New York City? Sex in the city; huh? What city. Black men are white men in New York City. The fuck whoever they want to. Don't give me shit about TV. This is not Miracle City. [turns violently towards the back] This must be violating some law.

DR. REMINGTON
Which one?

KATYDID
If they made a law for mothers, parents in distress to be able to drop off new babies at the hospital instead of into the dumpsters, there must be a law about this.

DR. REMINGTON
It's not even possible, what's taken place with Charlie. It defies science, so it's beyond law.

KATYDID
Uh, I hate to inform you, Dr. with all your brainpower, not if he's black.
[Lights fade. Shadows on Charles Free stands up, walks up as if its a podium.]

CHARLES
I thank my mother I also thank the grandmothers all 3.1596 million who are taking care of my black babies. I thank God these blessings are all from the man upstairs. I thank a free market economy that I can sell my black talent to the highest bidder, Sony, Atlantic, Death Row, Warner. I thank all my the poor down trodden unlucky, hard-working, sacrificing bearing up under incredible shit foremothers & fathers whose dead shoulders I'm not standing on because I'd rather be an ungrateful midget than upstandingly grateful. I thank all those fine gods who perfected capitalism. Henry Ford, who made it possible for me to be standing here crying and sweating I

thank NAACP and Essence & Soul Train for the sincerest form of flattery– imitation without which we couldn't be here, aping the whole corny narcissism, the unjokes unfunny emcees the elaborate amounts of money – - all spent on showing off the toys Barbie clothes in this floorshow tonight. I am so proud to be a member of this profession. Just think: Martin Luther King took a bullet for this Thank you God. Oh man. What a trip. If only I had stayed around long enough to get my boys tight. Death, you a motherfucker. And I didn't even leave no babies. Damn, wuzzup with that?

KATYDID
Somebody somewhere somehow tell me what is it? I can't stand it any longer. [Shadows engulf her. Nurses emerge]

ABYSINTHE
I don't care who the babydaddy. I welcome all these babies what come here without. They belong to us. We need a moment of silence. A moment of silence. More silence. More.

KATYDID
This is a Mexican stand off. Tell me the truth.

DR. REMINGTON
No.

KATYDID
What's happening?

DR. REMINGTON
No.

KATYDID
What is that thing? It's going to be the death of her if we don't find out what it is & why it is.

DR. REMINGTON
No.

KATYDID
How dare you, you white mother fucker.

DR. REMINGTON
No

KATYDID
What is it? A damn duck personduck doodlyduck a boy a damn thing that's here that's out of our control? What is it?

REGINA:
Charlie, I want you to look at this
[she pops a tape in the VCR; it plays on the back wall of stage; it's a still from Fellini's "Satyricon" showing grotesqueries, dwarves, etc.]
Look, Charlie. Freak is just a word for "I don't know you." But I know you, Charlie Quick Quack. Like my own child.
[Lots of splashing in the pool. Regina thrashes around as if chasing Charlie]
Charlie, you must look at this. Don't be disgusted
[she is drenched by the splashing].
I am not disgusted. I love you
-[she sits down]

KATYDID
When I took Jo-Jo to see the live Barney in the auditorium, the same thing. I tell you, those little kids were so excited. They had their little purple Barney toys and they were singing that goofy song [sings a few notes] and all their mothers or aunties or grandmas– maybe one or two baby daddies in the crowd- had them all ready to see Barney. And I mean, this great big huge Barney-looked like a dinosaur with purple carpeting- comes out and all the kids starting crying. I mean bawling, and shivering and boo-hooing. They were scared shitless. Jo-Jo jumped on my chest and I could feel his little heart thumping away. He was terrified. It was one thing to see Barney on the TV set everyday of their lives & a horse of a different color to see this great big old purple people-eating mega-saurus. They never did get those kids quieted down. The closer he came to them, they freaked out completely. No. No. No. Everything doesn't need to be confronted directly... TV is the painless way.

REGINA
[Regina touches the remote and the VCR clicks on forward. Image after image slowly fill the stage. They're all of black people of real tall black athletes, of Africans, of African-Americans of Venus, Marcus Garvey. Venus Hottentot, Harret Tubman,] Charlie, they've called us freaks since they brought us here. Freaks niggahs darkies platypus mouth ugly pea-brained spooks mammies uncle toms whores hos stunted the underclass hooligans thugs...but we just keep on going down Life Street Who's going to stop you?
[two meds outside hospital; INCH sign glows in the dark. Carlights shoot by. Sirens.]

MED 1
Did you get the mother's permission? The next of kin? His mother works here.

MED 1
One moment [they waited, suspended for a moment]

MED 2
[To the audience]... Did he say a moment or minute?

MED 1
Oh, you used to watch "My Little Margie."

MED 2
Remember Gale Storm would say, "I'll be back in a minute."

MED 1
No, no, no, she said, "I'll be back in a moment."

MED 2
How old are you anyway?

MED 1
I was born before black people had pictures of the holy trinity on their wall.

MED 2
Martin Luther King, Kennedy, Malcolm X?

MED 1
No, no, no, Martin Luther King, Kennedy, Jesus.

MED 2
You're wrong. Martin Luther King, Gandhi, Kennedy.

MED 1
Kennedy, King & Garvey. Go me one.[They keep arguing until they come to blows, tussling until they fall and knock each other out.]

END PLAY

Monologues

EX-SLAVE

massa were a kind person when he felt like it…it were his chiren who were mean as snakes…and I were a house nigga…no pribilege…you jest closer to harm…see this here disfigurity …massa's little boy was a rocking his chair…a rocking in his chair…dat was de same ole chair I rocked him… when he were a baby… and I were cleaning the floor on mah hands…and my knees…and my skirts got caught in the rocker… and I fell under de wooden curve…right under de wooden curve… and it crushed mah face… it were a broken jaw…that massa never got fixed…never took me to de doctor…never even gave a fixing for it…sally the cook gave me uh ice chunk…to put upside it…and a plate of collard greens… which I couldn't chew…but I drank de pot likker…and so mah jaw look funny … mah jaw look funny…mah jaw look funny…but all de slaves had somepin like that…so nobody paid it any mind… but after de slavery I moved to de up nort… then I walked down de street…people stare at mah face…and turnt away…but don't bother me none…cuz it weren't mah fault…but when I read in de paper bout de plane crash…oh we was taught to read…after duh slavery…it were mah most precious thing… learning to read…and when I read about dah plane crashing out of dat sky…I say to myself…I hope massa's little boy done growed up… and caught dat plane…or his chirens on it….or they chirens on it…or somebody else's chirens on it…cuz god don't like ugly…and slavery was ugly… just as ugly as mah jaw…that broked and weren't never fixed…

MAX.

That's what I like about white people. They keep the same name generation after generation, Max, Max, Max, Max, Henry the first, Henry the second, Henry the eighth. They names is not confusing. They don't care if the little baby look up at em all funny, like Mabel? Why you giving me this tired name again? We do different. We go whichever way we get enslaved. Wha massa name? John? Das my name. We get with the French and we name ourselves Denise, Charmaine, Elouise. We get with the Irish and it's Siobhan, Mickey. We went Swahili, evbody had Cumbuka, emboli-all them names sound like they got booger or booty up in em. Haki Madhubootie. So now we got all these twenty somethings running around with Ay-rab names. Ahmed, Muhammad, Siddiqi.They just sounded different before Sept. 11: Khalid, Abdul, and Hasan.Now it sounds like your grandson is on the 22 Most Wanted List. And if you go to the Post Office and look at the faces, you don't see Amad al-sheik Abdullah. You see Miz Jones' nephew what been living with her since he got out of prison. Or Tommy Green who six feet eight and cain't play basketball. And white folks still naming babies Thomas and Jefferson and George. And here An test. The Mexicans never enslaved us but show me a black baby name José.

ANN AND EMMETT TILL

I grew up on Emmett Till and JET magazine. Since when did folks get so fucking innocent they can't see blood and suffering? JET was the only place that would publish the burnt up corpses of the lynched Negroes the only place where you could see Emmett Till body all laid up in the funeral home where his mama said Let the whole world see what they done to my boy As I recall, some folk used to hold lynch parties make picture postcards out of the poor burnt up bodies. some folks mean as snakes

ANN AND THE NAMIBIANS

You can be picky when you got it good. I had it good. Ann didn't always be out here like a wild dog. I had a house and a family. My luck got bad and then it disappeared. Nobody wants ya when ya down and out. You need to meet the Namibis…I saw these Namibi refugees on TV. Black as midnight. So black they were blue. Beautiful. Stunning Black. And a white lady from Paly Alto was showing them around a park, a nice, big walking and jogging park down there near Stanford. And she was just a showing them how to go walking in this trail that was all winding and getting into darkness. And one of them Namibis said, "Will I get eaten if I go in there?" Ain't that nice? Afraid of lions and tigers. We not afraida lions and tigers. We got bigger problems. Wait till he gets pestered to death walking past the homeless. Funk. Dirt. We more scared of dirt than lions and tigers. We got guns and zoos. We tame wild animals. I got things worse than funk. But if you never get to know me, you'll never find em.

ANN ON UNEMPLOYMENT

Negroes don't wont jobs, they don't wont full employment. Unemployment is self-medication for Negroes. We get fired, "Fuck it. I didn't want this job no way." We would go stark raving mad if all us had to work every day. That demands yo attention. And Negroes don't wanna pay attention cuz when they do they damn near trampled into extinction. We better off unemployed. And Ann a prime example. Ann not drowning in credit-card debt. Ann don't have no phone to get turned off. Ann mortgage not worrying her to death. And Ann not getting high blood from trying to keep up with the Joneses. And Ann ain't had a job since Hector was a pup.

ANN GOES TO CHURCH

A white woman I know, one a my buddies...she big, got dishwater hair. On Sunday, she go up and down where the black churches are. First she go inside the open front door and estimate where in the service the pastor is. She know bout call and response. She know where the climax. Then she walks out wif her cane and her waddle. She bold. She go round the back door and check to see if it's a feast waiting for the Sunday go-to-meeting folk. Cuz she know bout black churches. [starts singing "Amazing Grace"] A-maz, white folk church over, Zing, White folk be out the door, Grace, white folk be at the Sizzler eating dinner, How Sweet, it Monday morn, white folk at work, The sound, white folk be done got they paycheck and black folk still in church. And she help herself and keep on down the street, as resolute as a street dog. She been doing this for years, say her only good meal is on Sunday morning in the black community.

GODZILLA OF INNOCENCE

How did white Americans get so innocent? Why do they hate us? Why would they kill innocent people? A while back a white woman went to get her prescription filled in the middle of the night in Oakland on Telegraph Ave. Now that's bad enough right there. As a black woman I would be watching my back just on account of that. But this woman-God rest her innocent pure soul-takes her recycling to the back of the Walgreen's at midnight after getting her prescription filled. I know she must have been in pain to be out at that time of night but as luck would have it a crackhead comes up and blows her away. Very sad but, again I ask, when did white folks get so fucking innocent? With the blood of four centuries of oppression and war and what do you call that when you take somebody's land and call it your own –appropriation, misappropriation? And I know white folks love to say, but I never owned slaves I never did that That was over 150 years ago. I grew up in East Oakland I was never a slave I never picked cotton or got paid in chittlins and hog maw but I know from whence I came and the road that led here. And here we go again with this guy in the CIA, this innocence this fucking innocence. Why? Johnny Mike Spann. He was 29 years old. Wanted to be in the CIA or FBI since high school. Where did he get this notion? Only two of two places: movies and tv. He was watching reruns of "The Man from U.N.C.L.E." and "The Saint" with Roger Moore, not to mention Tarzan, the original CIA, the template for the CIA, Bwana. This was the pattern in his little blond head. That's why two CIA, with their pistols, he's so proud to be one of them-step up in front of a crowd of captured Taliban with a simple-assed question, Why are you here? A real John Wayne moment on non-John Wayne turf. Of course all hell breaks loose and while Spann kills three of them, they stomp and bite, yes, bite, yes, bite him to death. "Mission Impossible" never ended like that. "Secret Agent" man? It's very powerful when our fantasies come true. It's very dangerous when our fantasies come true because it's very unreal when our fantasies come true.

ELVIS RIPPED OFF BIG MOMMA
Thornton...The hound dog...Jughead was an agent provocateur for the FBI...Millie the model had silicone implants but we didn't want to hear it...Yeah...True Romance tears stop where the real ones start...Ike was a colored man...Dinah Shore's a fugitive from the Negro race...Sammy Davis, Jr. got that empty eye socket from the mob...Little Lotta's fat comes from the diethylstilbestrol in all those hamburgers she stuffs down her fat white gut...Even if we heard it, it would have gone in one ear and out the other...Archie and Veronica freaked on her daddy's bed...You gotta use your imagination, otherwise you'll just be thinking some guy is peeing inside you... Richie Rich made his money from black sugar workers in rural Cuba...Louie Louie was a flasher...Nkrumah led Ghana into the future fabulous

KATYDID'S SOLILOQUY

I'm worried about my big sistah, a pediatric nurse. Don't know if she's paying her rent on time. Her landlord is the nicest person in the world. But gratitude turns on a dime. Always on call, on duty working her tail off. Devoting her entire life to NICU. It's crazy to be up in her hospital. You couldn't pay me to work here. Why? What for? Story of her life. Work, work, work, work, work, work. She's gonna work so hard she loses her mind? And the next thing you know she's homeless. I hate the homeless especially when they're black. That's a modern redundancy. We've been homeless for 400 years. Six months ago, I took my unemployment and gave them a bullshit story about getting a job in New York City. If I was out of work, why not see the world while I'm at it. And I learned about black people being homeless. I'm walking from the "Y" to the half-price ticket booth to see CATS, Times Square with all the tourists and garment factory workers and homeless who, I'd like to say, in New York City have a NIMBY attitude. The homeless in Oaktown so passive they're for real for real begging. They have the pleading posture. They work on empathy here. That don't play in New York. They have the managerial homeless in Manhattan. Mental but managing it, they know how and when to go crazy. How and when to get in your face. I may not know Karate but I know Ka-razy. Being homeless in New York is about real estate, baby. Location, Location, Location. In Oaktown they position themselves on the edge of the corner as if to say, I'm on the edge... help me!! I'm falling. In New York, they're in the middle of the sidewalk. I was going to a Knicks game at Madison Square Garden. Do you think this guy could have rolled himself up so I wouldn't have to step over him? Puh!! I don't think so. They occupy their turf and you're just an invader. "Gimme some money bitch....I know you got some money...Gimme some...Well get on out of here, black bitch." The energy. They work the streets there. Here, I've seen this same guy- blond scruffy hair, in fatigues for three years, near the freeway. Same sign: Will work for food. Same silent plea. Bro, if you were going over the edge you would have gone. But my biggest fright was outside this quasi-upscale Berkeley supermarket. A black woman like me, my brown skinned doppelganger, school teacher-ish, dressed in London fog raincoat, looking like my kind– you know how you pass somebody on the street and think we're the same station in life– and she approached me. Can you give me some money? Whoa. I know you can make a living like that. They can make $50, even more, a day if they persist. But I thought: What if I end up like her? I'm good with signs. But what am I going to do? Be like the New Yorkers or the ones here?

THE ANTI-VAGABONDS

Sometimes I sit near Lake Merritt when the sun's out and I ask myself, why do I keep seeing the dark side, the underbelly of California? The answers to that question lead me to the underbelly. One answer is that, having left the state after being a black activist and Black Panther, I came back on the tail end of a magnificent drug war. My parents' house in East Oakland was a stone's throw from the site of Felix Mitchell's drug operation. There I sat, night after night, listening to the sound track of urban warfare– gunshots, sirens, ambulances. Another reason–I'm the child of Oklahomans who migrated West in the 30s and 40s to escape segregation and fill wartime jobs. As a child I heard their stories as tall tales: Each relative arrived at the Santa Fe terminus in Berkeley, shepherded from down south by kindly Pullman Porters, eating fried chicken and pound cake packed neatly in wax paper since they couldn't use the dining car down south. They saved down payments in Mason jars for the two bedroom bungalows in Oakland, Berkeley, and Richmond. Granddad was one of Oklahoma's first black oil millionaires, a piece of family that Dad told Mom we didn't need to know about. Dad was a Tuskegee Airman, 332nd Fighter Group, his CO, Benjamin O. Davis. He kept getting mistaken for The Brown Bomber Joe Louis. Mom and Dad owned the only black taxicab company in Berkeley in the 40s. My parents were told to Go Home after the war. They told a lot of black people that. But we weren't going anywhere. My great uncle Walter might be the third reason. He was my grandmother's brother, who took a bride, Emily, in Muskogee. Emily, who could have passed for white but didn't. The day they married, a white man ran to Walter's house, told him a mob was on its way to lynch him for marrying Emily, and he'd better catch the next train running. You bet he did. He and Emily settled in Joplin, Missouri. After Emily passed, Uncle Walter married Aunt Fanny who had a little boy named Garvin who grew up to become Lt. Col. Garvin A. Tutt, Buffalo soldier, 92nd infantry. As kids, we'd pile into the Ford Fairlane and visit Garvin and his family at The Presidio in San Francisco. While he and Dad yakked, we played with his daughters, one of whom, Barbara, grew up to become Congresswoman Barbara Lee. I hope you get that Anti-vagabond theme here. I came home to my aging parents. I understood they had fought the sordid underbelly their whole time in Cali. Humph. Their whole lives.

THE ELEPHANTS: AN OPPRESSION STORY

Well into the 2000s, black people in California cities tired of whites, Asians and various assorted others moving them out of the urban grid and building high priced hi-tech residences. In their tiredness, blacks noticed that the invasioneers came with multitudes of dogs. In Oakland, the invasioneers walked these dogs day and night. This was irritating in one sense because the blacks felt inconsequential enough against the forces of gentrification. It infuriated others who felt minimized for another reason. These dogs were treated tenderly though leashed. Allowed to stop and smell the flowers and nibble the dirt. Kindly permitted to urinate at will. Lovingly waited upon as they assimilated expensive doggie treats and expelled the detritus. The women of one black book group fumed at this [for them] intellectual dilemma. They owned aging homes in the flatlands of East Oakland and South Berkeley. Their primary financial burdens were poorer relatives who had had to vacate rentals with five day notices and move to towns like Antioch, Stockton and Vallejo. And not the nicer parts of these Joaquin towns. As a nonblack book selection– in an annual nod at diversity– the ladies had read Guns, Germs and Steel by Jared Diamond. They found its inevitable link to their own mission when they got to the chapters which theorized why the African continent hadn't prospered in the centuries moving toward the millennium. It was very simple, though it took hundreds of pages to explicate: the Africans hadn't domesticated lions, tigers, elephants and the like. Unlike the horses, cattle, wolves, sheep on other continents, Diamond argued, the big kills of the savannahs provided food and hide to sustain the hunter/food gatherers for long periods of time. One woman, incensed at driving two hours each way by herself to Manteca to see family, wished out loud. If the Africans had domesticated the elephant the way that dogs had evolved from wolves, I could have my baby elephant right here at my feet, no bigger than a chihuahua. In the spirit of the club, one wanted the elephant for a service animal. What if Oscar Grant had been accompanied through Fruitvale Station by an elephant evolved down to counter oppression that fateful New Year's Eve? What of an Oakland populated by residents adorned with priceless ivory, fond mementos of their deceased pets? As they rhapsodized this fantasy into Oaklanders walking around its fabulous manmade lake with reductive elephants and ivory arm chains instead of slabs of ribs and BBQ sauce, the naysayer/naturalist in the group offered her parting thought: we would become the captors and minimizers of one of the world's most incredible natural wonders. Where Diamond presents his theory as objective fact, I say predators indulgently turned gifts from nature into beasts of burden while others hunted only out of necessity.

The pragmatic founder of the club, whose 3bd/2.5ba was an Airbnb while she stayed at her grandson's in Tracy, wrapped it up: our next selection is DeFacto Feminism: Essays Straight Outta Oakland by Judy Juanita. It has a ghost story that's a wild and wooly mammoth for you elephant mystics. See you next month.

Judy Juanita's Plays: A Performance History

Full length and one-acts

"Life is a Carousel" (full-length play about a forgotten founder of black studies). Directed by Edris Cooper Anifowoshe, Brava! Theater, SF, staged reading, November, 2015. Readers Theater, Oakland Public Library, February 2015. Directed by Judy Juanita.

"Counter-Terrorism" (one-act: two women, one homeless, one bourgeois, react to 9/11 and war on terrorism), production November 2008, at The Marsh, SF.2002-2005, at Laney & Holy Names Colleges & Loyola Marymount University, at the Bay Area Playwrights Festival 2004, at SF's Off-Market Theater.

"Theodicy" a full-length play about two old coots who step into the river of death. Developmental reading, 2006 & staged reading, 2007, Playwrights Center San Francisco, Off-Market Theatre. 2nd place (of 186 full-length plays) in 2007 Eileen Heckart Drama Competition. Reading, Ohio State University, 2008.

"A Moment of Silence" (one-act satire about cloning set at a children's hospital) Production, Laney College English Dept., 2006.

"Knocked Up," co-written with Tina Murch, (one-act commedia dell'Arte: on the RU486 pill), toured Northern California venues and colleges 1993-1995 productions by the SF Mime Troupe, including a Mission Cultural Center production directed by Michael Sullivan. Production, Humboldt State University Summer Arts Program & SF Mime Troupe, 2006.

"Heaven's Hold" (full-length: black girl in Oakland in the fifties wins essay contest on Americanism) produced at Brava! Theatre's New Play Festival in 1992 in S.F., and staged at the National Black Theater Festival in Winston-Salem, NC. 2001.

"The Kinship" (full-length: oral history in a prominent black Oakland family) month-long run at NYC's Basement Workshop; Ernest Abuba directed, 1986.

10 minute

"Schooldays," (10-minute play about condescension and the use of the n-word by college students) produced at Woman's Will 24-hour Playfest at the Julia Morgan Theater for the Performing Arts in Berkeley, 2009.

"The Art of Benevolence," (10-minute play about kindness) produced at Woman's Will 24-hour Playfest at the Julia Morgan Theater for the Performing Arts in Berkeley, 2008.

"The History of Sweat," " (10-minute play about fragrance and subways) produced at Woman's Will 24-hour Playfest at the Julia Morgan Theater for the Performing Arts in Berkeley, 2007.

"Life is a Carousel" (10-minute play about a forgotten founder of black studies). Directed by Suze Allen. Mid America Theatre Conference, Minneapolis, 2007. Staged reading, Marsh Café, San Francisco, 2006.

"Famine" (10-minute farce about one of the seven deadly sins) produced at the Woman's Will 24-hour Playfest at the Julia Morgan Theater for the Performing Arts in Berkeley, 2006.

"All it takes is one" (10-minute farce about charitable intentions) produced at the Woman's Will 24-hour Playfest at the Julia Morgan Theater for the Performing Arts in Berkeley, 2005. Production, Laney College English Dept. 2006.

"Fat Women at Lunch" (10-minute satire on weight and sexuality) performed at Womanbooks, NYC, 1986, published in 2003 in the literary quarterly Rooms

Other Books by Judy Juanita

Novelist, poet, and essayist Judy Juanita's latest poetry collection, *Gawdzilla*, (EquiDistance, 2022) conflates the destructive, prehistoric sea monster Godzilla with U.S. imperialism and racism. Her debut poetry collection, *Manhattan my ass, you're in Oakland*, (EquiDistance, 2021) won the American Book Award from the Before Columbus Foundation in 2021. In her semi-autobiographical novel, *Virgin Soul* (Viking, 2013); its protagonist joins the Black Panther Party in the sixties in the San Francisco-Oakland Bay Area. Her collection of short stories, *The High Price of Freeways*, won the 2021 Tartt Fiction Award, (Livingston Press, 2022). Her collection of essays, *DeFacto Feminism: Essays Straight Outta Oakland* (EquiDistance, 2016), examines race, gender, politics, and spirituality, as experienced by a black activist and self-described "feminist foot soldier." Her work achieved Pushcart Prize nominations for (poem) "Bling" 2012; (essay) "The Gun as Performance Poem" 2014; and (short story) "The Black House" 2022. She teaches writing at the University of California, Berkeley.

www.ingramcontent.com/pod-product-compliance
Lightning Source LLC
Chambersburg PA
CBHW081358290426
44110CB00018B/2414